PERSONALIZED COMPUTATIONAL SKILLS PROGRAM

Bryce R. Shaw

MODULE C
DECIMALS, PROPORTIONS, AND PERCENTS

UNIT 10   **Decimals**
UNIT 11   **Proportions**
UNIT 12   **Percents**

Houghton Mifflin Company, Boston

Dallas   Geneva, Illinois   Hopewell, New Jersey

Palo Alto   London

Credits and Copyright

AUTHOR

Bryce R. Shaw

CONTRIBUTING AUTHOR

Linda M. Oldaker, Arizona State University

ADVISERS

Ernest J. Cioffi, University of Southern California
Sandra Pryor Clarkson, Hunter College, New York
Gwen Shelton, Bee College, Texas

AUTHOR'S PREFACE

I wish to acknowledge the contribution of the many students and instructors whose cooperation and support over the past fifteen years made possible the research and analysis that was essential to the development of the PERSONALIZED COMPUTATIONAL SKILLS PROGRAM. To them, I dedicate this program.

I also wish to acknowledge the contribution of the many individuals in the College Division at Houghton Mifflin Company whose total effort made the publication of this work possible. To them, I express my sincere appreciation.

For all of the individuals responsible for this publication, I express our mutual hope that this program will be successful in reaching its goal of helping ever greater numbers of students master those mathematics skills that are essential for a productive and rewarding adult life.

B. R. S.

Program Contents

MODULE A   **WHOLE NUMBERS**   **1**

List of Objectives and BRUSH-UP Record   6
Module Diagnostic Test   9

UNIT 1   WHOLE NUMBERS: ADDITION   11
UNIT 2   WHOLE NUMBERS: SUBTRACTION   47
UNIT 3   WHOLE NUMBERS: MULTIPLICATION   89
UNIT 4   WHOLE NUMBERS: DIVISION   143

Module Mastery Test   187

MODULE B   **FRACTIONS**   **193**

List of Objectives and BRUSH-UP Record   198
Module Diagnostic Test   201

UNIT 5   FRACTIONS: BASIC SKILLS   203
UNIT 6   FRACTIONS: ADDITION   261
UNIT 7   FRACTIONS: SUBTRACTION   291
UNIT 8   FRACTIONS: MULTIPLICATION   327
UNIT 9   FRACTIONS: DIVISION   351

Module Mastery Test   379

MODULE C   **DECIMALS, PROPORTIONS, PERCENTS**   **385**

List of Objectives and BRUSH-UP Record   390
Module Diagnostic Test   393

UNIT 10   DECIMALS   395
UNIT 11   PROPORTIONS   453
UNIT 12   PERCENTS   487

Module Mastery Test   539

The Program and How to Use It

WHAT IS PCSP?

The PERSONALIZED COMPUTATIONAL SKILLS PROGRAM is an instructional program uniquely designed to meet the special needs of mature students who desire to improve their proficiency with the 105 computational skills most needed for adult life and continued study. PCSP is ideally suited for use as a text in college review courses. It will also function well in math tutorial lab situations. It may even be used as a self-help program.

PCSP is organized into three modules: Module A reviews addition, subtraction, multiplication, and division of whole numbers; Module B covers fractions; and Module C deals with decimals, proportions, and percents.

WHO NEEDS PCSP?

Any adult who has been away from math for a time can use the PERSONALIZED COMPUTATIONAL SKILLS PROGRAM to brush up forgotten skills. Recent studies show that most adults do forget some of the computational skills they once learned if they have not been using them. For example, many people have difficulty remembering what to do in order to solve each of the three types of problems involving percents.

Among those who will find PCSP *most* beneficial is the person who is going on to college, perhaps after a time away from formal schooling. For this individual, PCSP will help restore confidence and eliminate math anxiety by providing the opportunity to refresh essential skills prerequisite for future coursework.

WHY IS PCSP UNIQUE?

The problem for most adult students is that they need to review some skills, but not all. The problem is compounded for their instructors, for in any given class different students will have different review needs. Despite these realities, most existing programs force both students and instructors to begin at the beginning and needlessly review everything in sight. As a consequence, the time available in a one-semester review course is too often consumed by an exhaustive review of the whole numbers at the expense of a more needed review of fractions, decimals, and percents.

The PERSONALIZED COMPUTATIONAL SKILLS PROGRAM uniquely solves this problem. PCSP is organized around a series of self-checking Diagnostic and Mastery Tests that permit the student to identify precisely (on an objective-by-objective basis) which skills need to be reviewed and which do not. Thus the student can use available time to concentrate on those areas of greatest need. The diagnostic and review process is not only more efficient but more comfortable as well.

HOW DOES PCSP WORK?

The form of PCSP is determined by the need that it is designed to serve. The first goal is to pinpoint review needs in a sequential and orderly way. Therefore, the essential organizer of the program is a series of self-checking DIAGNOSTIC TESTS which begin each of the 12 units in the program. These tests check the mastery level for each skill in a given unit on an objective-by-objective basis. When test results reveal a review need, the student can proceed *directly* to the appropriate LESSON on that skill and then on to the associated PRACTICE pages. When all necessary work in the unit has been completed, the student can check his or her new mastery level (again, on an objective-by-objective basis) using the self-checking MASTERY TEST at the end of the unit.

The process looks like this:

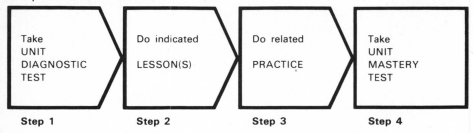

| Take UNIT DIAGNOSTIC TEST | Do indicated LESSON(S) | Do related PRACTICE | Take UNIT MASTERY TEST |
| Step 1 | Step 2 | Step 3 | Step 4 |

There is a very important relationship between the three items that test a given skill on the TEST pages, the three Worked Examples for the same skill on the LESSON page, and the problems on the PRACTICE pages that follow. The three test items define three levels of difficulty within the skill, and these levels of difficulty are faithfully followed in the Brush-up Exercises on the LESSON pages and in the drill on the subsequent PRACTICE pages.

In order to make progress through the program more efficient, the following criteria are suggested:

TEST ITEMS CORRECT	ASSIGNMENT
3 out of 3	Skip LESSON entirely
2 out of 3	Do LESSON (with Brush-up Exercises) only
1 out of 3	Do LESSON plus PRACTICE (odd numbers)
0 out of 3	Do LESSON plus PRACTICE (all problems)

OTHER FEATURES

Module Tests   Each PCSP module is also bracketed by a MODULE DIAGNOSTIC TEST and a MODULE MASTERY TEST. These tests are especially useful when the student feels reasonably secure with the content of a given module in advance of instruction. These tests may indicate that a given module (or units within a module) may be skipped entirely.

Record-keeping Charts   A combined CONTENTS AND BRUSH-UP RECORD will be found at the beginning of each module. These pages list all of the skill objectives for each of the units within the module and simultaneously provide columns for "Work Needed" and for checking it off when completed. These pages are useful both as an instructional management tool and as a permanent record of progress and accomplishment.

Instructor's Manual   An Instructor's Manual is available to accompany the PERSONALIZED COMPUTATIONAL SKILLS PROGRAM. The manual provides the instructor with a complete battery of alternate DIAGNOSTIC and MASTERY TESTS for the entire program on 60 "permission-to-reproduce" pages. In addition, a PROGRAM DIAGNOSTIC TEST and a PROGRAM MASTERY TEST are provided. These may be used respectively as a program placement test at the beginning of the course and as a final exam at the end of the course.

Module C

Contents and BRUSH-UP Record

UNIT 10 DECIMALS		PAGE	SCORE	WORK NEEDED	(✔)
UNIT DIAGNOSTIC TEST		397			
Skill 1	Write decimals to ten-thousandths.	399			
Skill 2	Round decimals to the nearest tenth, hundredth, and thousandth.	403			
Skill 3	Write whole numbers, fractions, and mixed numbers as decimals.	407			
Skill 4	Write decimals as fractions and mixed numbers.	411			
REVIEW: Skills 1–4		414			
Skill 5	Add decimals to ten-thousandths with no regrouping.	415			
Skill 6	Add decimals to ten-thousandths with regrouping.	419			
Skill 7	Subtract decimals to ten-thousandths with no regrouping.	423			
Skill 8	Subtract decimals to ten-thousandths with regrouping.	427			
REVIEW: Skills 5–8		432			
Skill 9	Multiply a decimal by a whole number.	433			
Skill 10	Multiply a decimal by a decimal.	437			
Skill 11	Divide a decimal by a whole number.	441			
Skill 12	Divide a decimal by a decimal.	445			
REVIEW: Skills 9–12		450			
UNIT MASTERY TEST		451			

UNIT 11 PROPORTIONS	PAGE	SCORE	WORK NEEDED	(✔)
UNIT DIAGNOSTIC TEST	455			
Skill 1 Write ratios in simplest form, using "TO", a colon (:), or a fraction.	457			
Skill 2 Write rates in simplest form, using a fraction.	461			
Skill 3 Find unit rates.	465			
REVIEW: Skills 1–3	470			
Skill 4 Determine if proportions are true.	471			
Skill 5 Solve true proportions.	475			
Skill 6 Write equal rates as a proportion, then solve.	479			
REVIEW: Skills 4–6	484			
UNIT MASTERY TEST	485			

UNIT 12 PERCENTS	PAGE	SCORE	WORK NEEDED	(✔)
UNIT DIAGNOSTIC TEST	489			
Skill 1 Rewrite whole number percents up to 100% in fractional or decimal form.	491			
Skill 2 Rewrite whole number percents larger than 100% in fractional or decimal form.	493			
Skill 3 Rewrite percents less than 1% in fractional or decimal form.	497			
Skill 4 Rewrite mixed number and decimal percents in fractional or decimal form.	501			
REVIEW: Skills 1–4	506			
Skill 5 Rewrite decimals as percents.	507			
Skill 6 Rewrite fractions as percents.	511			
Skill 7 Rewrite whole numbers and mixed numbers as percents.	515			
REVIEW: Skills 5–7	518			

UNIT 12 (Continued) PERCENTS	PAGE	SCORE	WORK NEEDED	(✔)
Skill 8 Find a percentage of a given number.	519			
Skill 9 Find what percent one number is of another number.	525			
Skill 10 Find a number if a percentage of the number is known.	531			
REVIEW: Skills 8–10	536			
UNIT MASTERY TEST	537			

DECIMALS, PROPORTIONS, AND PERCENTS

Module Diagnostic Test – Page 1

Answers on Page 541

UNIT 10   DECIMALS

SKILL 1 Write as a decimal.

10 and
18 thousandths

SKILL 2 Round to the nearest hundredth.

6.075

SKILL 3 Write as a decimal.

$9\frac{7}{100}$

SKILL 4 Write as a mixed number in lowest terms.

24.15

SKILL 5

$$3.914$$
$$+\ 72.07$$

SKILL 6

$$3.75$$
$$+\ 16.58$$

SKILL 7

$$28.395$$
$$-\ \ 2.17$$

SKILL 8

$$132.975$$
$$-\ \ \ \ 8.99$$

SKILL 9

$$29.7$$
$$\times\ 16$$

SKILL 10

$$27.38$$
$$\times\ 9.23$$

SKILL 11

$45\overline{)57.6}$

SKILL 12

$0.134\overline{)0.1809}$

UNIT 11   PROPORTIONS

SKILL 1 Write the ratio as a fraction in simplest form.

96 kg to 10 kg

SKILL 2 Write the rate in simplest form, using a fraction.

$90 for 8 hr

SKILL 3 Find the unit rate. Round to the nearest tenth.

58 mi in 6 min

UNIT 11

4.

5.

6.

UNIT 12

1.

2.

3.

4.

5.

6.

7.

8.

9.

10.

394

UNIT 11 PROPORTIONS

SKILL 4 Tell if the proportion is TRUE or NOT TRUE.

$$\frac{15}{18} \overset{?}{=} \frac{75}{90}$$

SKILL 5 Find the unknown value. Check the answer.

$$\frac{m}{32} = \frac{108}{192}$$

SKILL 6 Write and solve the proportion.

350 km in 8 hr
$= n$ km in 12 hr

UNIT 12 PERCENTS

SKILL 1 Write in fractional and decimal form.

55%

SKILL 2 Write in fractional and decimal form.

350%

SKILL 3 Write in fractional and decimal form.

0.15%

SKILL 4 Write in fractional and decimal form.

72.8%

SKILL 5 Write as a percent.

0.735

SKILL 6 Write as a percent.

$$\frac{7}{8}$$

SKILL 7 Write as a percent.

$$3\frac{2}{5}$$

SKILL 8 What is 118% of 95?

SKILL 9 What percent of 65 is 11.7?

SKILL 10 16.2 is 36% of what number?

UNIT 10
DECIMALS

Skill 1   Write decimals to ten-thousandths.

Skill 2   Round decimals to the nearest tenth, hundredth, and thousandth.

Skill 3   Write whole numbers, fractions, and mixed numbers as decimals.

Skill 4   Write decimals as fractions and mixed numbers.

Skill 5   Add decimals to ten-thousandths with no regrouping.

Skill 6   Add decimals to ten-thousandths with regrouping.

Skill 7   Subtract decimals to ten-thousandths with no regrouping.

Skill 8   Subtract decimals to ten-thousandths with regrouping.

Skill 9   Multiply a decimal by a whole number.

Skill 10   Multiply a decimal by a decimal.

Skill 11   Divide a decimal by a whole number.

Skill 12   Divide a decimal by a decimal.

Unit Diagnostic Test – Page 1

Answers on Page 541

SKILL 1   Write as decimals.

1. 6 and 3974 ten-thousandths

2. 2123 and 75 thousandths

3. six hundred one and nine hundredths

SKILL 2

1. Round 6.852 to the nearest hundredth.

2. Round 4.8711 to the nearest tenth.

3. Round 8.7196 to the nearest thousandth.

SKILL 3   Write as decimals.

1. $6\frac{3}{100}$

2. $\frac{13}{20}$

3. $5\frac{1}{9}$

SKILL 4   Write as a fraction or mixed number in lowest terms.

1. 0.050

2. 9.24

3. 8.027

SKILL 5

1. $\begin{array}{r} \$23.25 \\ +5.72 \\ \hline \end{array}$

2. $\begin{array}{r} 24.22 \\ 1.423 \\ +3.004 \\ \hline \end{array}$

3. 16.247 + 3.43

SKILL 6

1. $\begin{array}{r} \$46.28 \\ +64.80 \\ \hline \end{array}$

2. $\begin{array}{r} 46.624 \\ 9.34 \\ +162.566 \\ \hline \end{array}$

3. 674.72 + 89.483

SKILL 1

1.

2.

3.

SKILL 2

1.

2.

3.

SKILL 3

1.

2.

3.

SKILL 4

1.

2.

3.

SKILL 5

1.

2.

3.

SKILL 6

1.

2.

3.

397

SKILL 7

1.

2.

3.

SKILL 8

1.

2.

3.

SKILL 9

1.

2.

3.

SKILL 10

1.

2.

3.

SKILL 11

1.

2.

3.

SKILL 12

1.

2.

3.

SKILL 7

1. $\begin{array}{r} \$124.34 \\ -\ \ 12.21 \\ \hline \end{array}$

2. $\begin{array}{r} 167.246 \\ -\ \ 21.1 \\ \hline \end{array}$

3. $64.82 - 2.6$

SKILL 8

1. $\begin{array}{r} \$127.43 \\ -\ \ 68.54 \\ \hline \end{array}$

2. $\begin{array}{r} 307.4067 \\ -\ 127.6138 \\ \hline \end{array}$

3. $9.62 - 6.749$

SKILL 9

1. $\begin{array}{r} 4.06 \\ \times\ 7 \\ \hline \end{array}$

2. $\begin{array}{r} 27.13 \\ \times\ 43 \\ \hline \end{array}$

3. 129.173×105

SKILL 10

1. $\begin{array}{r} 26.12 \\ \times\ 0.2 \\ \hline \end{array}$

2. $\begin{array}{r} 18.11 \\ \times\ 3.04 \\ \hline \end{array}$

3. 125.50×0.219

SKILL 11

1. $72\overline{)345.6}$

2. $30\overline{)9.6}$

3. $0.4 \div 16$

SKILL 12

1. $0.23\overline{)1.633}$

2. $6.5\overline{)46.93}$

3. $107.42 \div 52.4$

OBJECTIVE   Skill 1   Write decimals to ten-thousandths.

SKILL MODEL

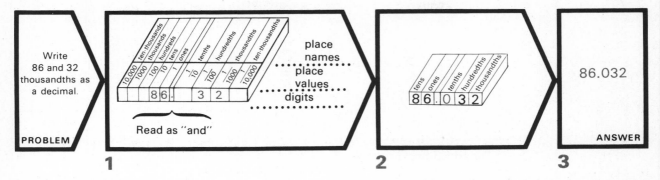

SOLUTION STEPS

Step 1 Write each whole number digit in the place-value chart. Then, starting with the last decimal digit (thousandths), write each decimal digit in the correct place.

Step 2 Write zeros in any blank places between the first and last digits.

Step 3 Write the decimal without the chart. Remember to copy the decimal point.

NOTE

When reading a decimal, the last digit tells you the place-value name.

0.0809 = [0 . 0 8 0 9]

0.0809 = 809 ten-thousandths

NOTE

If a decimal number is less than 1, write a 0 in the ones place.

Write 72 hundredths as 0.72

WORKED EXAMPLES

1. 5 and 682 thousandths

[5 . 6 8 2]

5.682

2. 302 and 4 hundredths

[3 0 2 . 0 4]

302.04

3. 5 thousand 3 and 7 ten-thousandths

[5 0 0 3 . 0 0 0 7]

5003.0007

BRUSH-UP EXERCISES

Write as decimals.

1. 32 hundredths

2. 8 and 74 hundredths

3. 104 thousandths

4. 4 and 6 tenths

5. 7 and 48 thousandths

6. 56 and 97 hundredths

7. 5 and 104 ten-thousandths

8. 40 and 9 ten-thousandths

SELF-CHECK ANSWERS

1. 0.32   **2.** 8.74   **3.** 0.104   **4.** 4.6   **5.** 7.048   **6.** 56.97

7. 54.0104   **8.** 40.0009

Read each decimal and write it in the place-value chart.
Remember AND separates the whole number from the decimal.

ANSWERS
1. 9.4
2. 9.53
3. 14.126
4. 68.4
5. 206.427
6. 104.9
7. 346.76
8. 147.204
9. 9.03
10. 0.8
11. 0.27
12. 0.07
13. 0.0117
14. 68.04
15. 0.017
16. 0.007
17. 206.0027
18. 206.007
19. 14.026
20. 14.0006
21. 60.004
22. 555.047
23. 263.0003

		hundreds	tens	ones	.	tenths	hundredths	thousandths	ten-thousandths
1.	9 and 4 tenths								
2.	9 and 53 hundredths								
3.	14 and 126 thousandths								
4.	68 and 4 tenths								
5.	206 and 427 thousandths								
6.	104 and 9 tenths								
7.	346 and 76 hundredths								
8.	147 and 204 thousandths								
9.	9 and 3 hundredths								
10.	8 tenths								
11.	27 hundredths								
12.	7 hundredths								
13.	117 ten-thousandths								
14.	68 and 4 hundredths								
15.	17 thousandths								
16.	7 thousandths								
17.	206 and 27 ten-thousandths								
18.	206 and 7 thousandths								
19.	14 and 26 thousandths								
20.	14 and 6 ten-thousandths								
21.	60 and 4 thousandths								
22.	555 and 47 thousandths								
23.	263 and 3 ten-thousandths								

PRACTICE　　　DECIMALS　　　Skill 1

Write each of the following as a decimal. Try to imagine a place-value chart as you write each.

1. 50 and 70 thousandths　　_____

2. 6 thousand and 8 hundredths　　_____

3. 5 and 22 thousandths　　_____

4. 18 and 701 ten-thousandths　　_____

5. 4 and 6 hundredths　　_____

6. 11 and 701 thousandths　　_____

7. 101 and 67 ten-thousandths　　_____

8. 8 thousand and 2 tenths　　_____

9. 1 and 1 ten-thousandth　　_____

10. 10 and 2 hundredths　　_____

11. 170 and 5 tenths　　_____

12. 63 and 4 thousandths　　_____

13. 54 and 16 ten-thousandths　　_____

14. 333 and 4 tenths　　_____

15. 290 and 5 hundredths　　_____

16. 111 and 201 thousandths　　_____

17. 5 and 5 ten-thousandths　　_____

18. 87 and 7 hundredths　　_____

19. 6 hundred and 5 hundredths　　_____

20. 902 and 7 thousandths　　_____

21. 7 thousand and 7 thousandths　　_____

22. 70 and 80 hundredths　　_____

23. 61 and 18 thousandths　　_____

ANSWERS

1. 50.070
2. 6000.08
3. 5.022
4. 18.0701
5. 4.06
6. 11.701
7. 101.0067
8. 8000.2
9. 1.0001
10. 10.02
11. 170.5
12. 63.004
13. 54.0016
14. 333.4
15. 290.05
16. 111.201
17. 5.0005
18. 87.07
19. 600.05
20. 902.007
21. 7000.007
22. 70.80
23. 61.018

Write each of the following as a decimal.

ANSWERS		
1. 0.40	**1.** forty hundredths	_____
2. 0.041	**2.** forty-one thousandths	_____
3. 0.403	**3.** four hundred three thousandths	_____
4. 0.008	**4.** eight thousandths	_____
5. 8.0027	**5.** eight and twenty-seven ten-thousandths	_____
6. 6.004	**6.** six and four thousandths	_____
7. 3.0703	**7.** three and seven hundred three ten-thousandths	_____
8. 40.602	**8.** forty and six hundred two thousandths	_____
9. 31.510	**9.** thirty-one and five hundred ten thousandths	_____
10. 9.0510	**10.** nine and five hundred ten ten-thousandths	_____
11. 503.05	**11.** five hundred three and five hundredths	_____
12. 500.35	**12.** five hundred and thirty-five hundredths	_____
13. 16.0025	**13.** sixteen and twenty-five ten-thousandths	_____
14. 5006.205	**14.** five thousand six and two hundred five thousandths	_____
15. 10.10	**15.** ten and ten hundredths	_____
16. 14.4	**16.** fourteen and four tenths	_____
17. 0.0003	**17.** three ten-thousandths	_____
18. 1.001	**18.** one and one thousandth	_____
19. 7007.007	**19.** seven thousand seven and seven thousandths	_____
20. 2.02	**20.** two and two hundredths	_____
21. 501.4	**21.** five hundred one and four tenths	_____
22. 11.0011	**22.** eleven and eleven ten-thousandths	_____
23. 316.006	**23.** three hundred sixteen and six thousandths	_____
24. 400.04	**24.** four hundred and four hundredths	_____
25. 8080.080	**25.** eight thousand eighty and eighty thousandths	_____

OBJECTIVE   Skill 2   Round decimals to the nearest
tenth, hundredth, and thousandth.

SKILL MODEL

Round 3.1278 to the nearest hundredth. **PROBLEM**	3.12	78 Given place (hundredths)	3.12	78 7 is more than 5	Drop ↓↑ 3.12	78 ──→ 3.13 ↑ Round up **ANSWER**
	1	**2**	**3A**

Round 5.3749 to the nearest hundredth.

5.37 | 49 ──────→ 5.37

4 is less than 5. Round down by dropping digits.

3B

SOLUTION STEPS

Step 1   Locate the digit in the given place (hundredths). Draw a line to its right.

Step 2   Decide if the first digit to the right of the line is 5 or more than 5.

Step 3A   If YES, "round up" by adding 1 to the digit in the given place. Drop the remaining digits to the right. This is the answer.

Step 3B   If NO, "round down" simply by dropping the digits to the right. This is the answer.

WORKED EXAMPLES

1. Round 1.34 to the nearest tenth.   1.3 | 4
Is 4 equal to 5 or more than 5?   NO
Answer: 1.3

2. Round 5.4864 to the nearest hundredth.   5.48 | 64
Is 6 equal to 5 or more than 5?   YES
Answer: 5.49

3. Round 17.8237 to the nearest thousandth.   17.823 | 7
Is 7 equal to 5 or more than 5?   YES
Answer: 17.824

BRUSH-UP EXERCISES

Round each number to the given place.

1. 8.43 to the nearest tenth

2. 4.30 to the nearest tenth

3. 6.7645 to the nearest hundredth

4. 18.3499 to the nearest hundredth

5. 0.8095 to the nearest thousandth

6. 9.1094 to the nearest thousandth

SELF-CHECK ANSWERS

1. 8.4   **2.** 4.3   **3.** 6.76   **4.** 18.35   **5.** 0.810   **6.** 9.109

PRACTICE

DECIMALS

Skill 2

Round each number to the nearest tenth and the nearest hundredth.

1. 4.2; 4.24

2. 67.8;
   67.84

3. 29.5;
   29.51

4. 146.8;
   146.83

5. 7.5; 7.46

6. 19.7;
   19.73

7. 4128.5;
   4128.45

8. 2674.0;
   2673.97

9. 600.3;
   600.26

10. 4003.5;
    4003.49

11. 4861.4;
    4861.39

12. 7326.1;
    7326.07

13. 24.1;
    24.11

14. 127.5;
    127.47

15. 1430.4;
    1430.38

		Nearest Tenth	Nearest Hundredth
1.	4.235		
2.	67.843		
3.	29.512		
4.	146.834		
5.	7.462		
6.	19.731		
7.	4128.452		
8.	2673.971		
9.	600.263		
10.	4003.485		
11.	4861.392		
12.	7326.072		
13.	24.1062		
14.	127.4650		
15.	1430.3785		

Copyright © 1980 by Houghton Mifflin Company. All rights reserved.

404

PRACTICE　　DECIMALS　　Skill 2

Round each number to the nearest tenth.

1. 8.96
2. 1.093
3. 8.74

4. 8.081
5. 8.79
6. 29.95

7. 28.049
8. 7.95
9. 1.23

10. 0.09
11. 3.94
12. 2.15

13. 3.83
14. 8.03
15. 2.46

Round each number to the nearest hundredth.

16. 7.895
17. 8.0065
18. 18.204

19. 16.921
20. 10.909
21. 0.009

22. 10.019
23. 6.375
24. 83.998

25. 9.991
26. 3.0009
27. 9.995

28. 21.780
29. 11.095
30. 0.995

Round each number to the nearest thousandth.

31. 2.0095
32. 3.8899
33. 0.0894

34. 6.0003
35. 1.0099
36. 1.0000

37. 2.0008
38. 2.4680
39. 0.0005

40. 16.0731
41. 7.6789
42. 9.8989

43. 1.9999
44. 4.4444
45. 9.9990

1. 9.0
2. 1.1
3. 8.7
4. 8.1
5. 8.8
6. 30.0
7. 28.0
8. 8.0
9. 1.2
10. 0.1
11. 3.9
12. 2.2
13. 3.8
14. 8.0
15. 2.5
16. 7.90
17. 8.01
18. 18.20
19. 16.92
20. 10.91
21. 0.01
22. 10.02
23. 6.38
24. 84.00
25. 9.99
26. 3.00
27. 10.00
28. 21.78
29. 11.10
30. 1.00
31. 2.010
32. 3.890
33. 0.089
34. 6.000
35. 1.010
36. 1.000
37. 2.001
38. 2.468
39. 0.001
40. 16.073
41. 7.679
42. 9.899
43. 2.000
44. 4.444
45. 9.999

405

ANSWERS

1. 6.3
2. 7.9
3. 8.7
4. 41.8
5. 564.6
6. 42.8
7. 1.18
8. 15.86
9. 37.42
10. 146.41
11. 124.35
12. 1.78
13. 4.53
14. 7.65
15. 5.47
16. 9.75
17. 63.12
18. 74.61
19. 19.18
20. 16.63
21. 28.45
22. 8.210
23. 34.746
24. 38.468
25. 42.401
26. 102.375
27. 0.268
28. 0.112
29. 0.348
30. 0.215
31. 0.428
32. 1.426
33. 4.542
34. 9.788
35. 6.342
36. 6.433
37. 67.011
38. 89.247
39. 14.143
40. 33.670
41. 28.454

WORKED EXAMPLE

Round 6.473 to the nearest hundredth.

6.47

Round each number to the nearest tenth.

1. 6.34   2. 7.92   3. 8.67

4. 41.782   5. 564.634   6. 42.79

Round each number to the nearest hundredth.

7. 1.178   8. 15.862   9. 37.416   10. 146.407   11. 124.350

12. 1.782   13. 4.525   14. 7.654   15. 5.467   16. 9.745

17. 63.1165   18. 74.6137   19. 19.1788   20. 16.6319   21. 28.4520

Round each number to the nearest thousandth.

22. 8.2103   23. 34.7461   24. 38.4678   25. 42.4011   26. 102.3745

27. 0.2679   28. 0.1115   29. 0.3475   30. 0.2154   31. 0.4278

32. 1.4256   33. 4.5422   34. 9.7875   35. 6.3421   36. 6.4325

37. 67.01145   38. 89.24668   39. 14.14257   40. 33.67012   41. 28.45429

OBJECTIVE   Skill 3   Write whole numbers, fractions, and mixed numbers as decimals.

SKILL MODEL

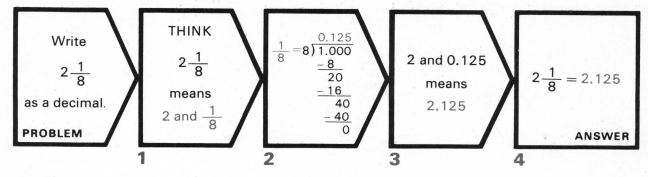

SOLUTION STEPS

Step 1   Think of the mixed number as a whole number and a fraction part.

Step 2   Divide the denominator of the fraction into the numerator. If necessary, round to the nearest thousandth.

Step 3   Combine the whole number and decimal.

Step 4   Write the answer.

> **NOTE**
>
> To write a whole number as a decimal, add a decimal point followed by one or more zeros.
>
> Write 4 as 4.0

WORKED EXAMPLES

1. $\dfrac{3}{4}$

$$\begin{array}{r} 0.75 \\ 4\overline{)3.00} \\ -2\,8 \\ \hline 20 \\ -20 \\ \hline 0 \end{array}$$

$\dfrac{3}{4} = 0.75$

2. $2\dfrac{1}{10}$

$2\dfrac{1}{10} = 2$ and $\dfrac{1}{10}$

$= 2$ and 0.1

$2\dfrac{1}{10} = 2.1$

3. $8\dfrac{2}{3} = 8$ and $\dfrac{2}{3}$

$\doteq 8$ and 0.667

$8\dfrac{2}{3} \doteq 8.667$

$$\begin{array}{r} 0.6666 \doteq 0.667 \\ 3\overline{)2.0000} \end{array}$$

The symbol $\doteq$ means "is approximately equal to". It is used when numbers are rounded.

BRUSH-UP EXERCISES

Write each number as a decimal. Round to the nearest thousandth if necessary.

1. $4\dfrac{8}{10}$ 2. $6\dfrac{3}{100}$ 3. $\dfrac{21}{1000}$ 4. $5\dfrac{3}{8}$

5. $4\dfrac{1}{4}$ 6. $1\dfrac{1}{8}$ 7. $3\dfrac{1}{9}$ 8. $\dfrac{2}{15}$

SELF-CHECK ANSWERS

1. 4.8   2. 6.03   3. 0.021   4. 5.375   5. 4.25   6. 1.125   7. 3.111   8. 0.133

407

ANSWERS
1. 0.125
2. 3.0
3. 0.0625
4. 34.0
5. 27.1875
6. 0.6875
7. 10.125
8. 0.1875
9. 21.9375
10. 0.3125
11. 0.25
12. 4.625
13. 0.5
14. 0.8125
15. 101.5625
16. 0.875
17. 27.25
18. 0.4375
19. 3.8125
20. 22.875
21. 43.0625
22. 90.75
23. 0.375
24. 9.6875
25. 0.75
26. 8.3125
27. 0.9375
28. 0.625
29. 0.5625
30. 7.4375

WORKED EXAMPLE

$$4\frac{3}{4} = 4 \text{ and } \frac{3}{4}$$
$$= 4 \text{ and } 0.75$$
$$= 4.75$$

$$4)\overline{3.00} \quad 0.75$$

Write each mixed number, whole number, or fraction as a decimal. Carry to four decimal places if necessary. Do not round answers.

1. $\frac{1}{8}$ **2.** 3

3. $\frac{1}{16}$ **4.** 34   **5.** $27\frac{3}{16}$ **6.** $\frac{11}{16}$

7. $10\frac{1}{8}$ **8.** $\frac{3}{16}$ **9.** $21\frac{15}{16}$ **10.** $\frac{5}{16}$

11. $\frac{1}{4}$ **12.** $4\frac{5}{8}$ **13.** $\frac{1}{2}$ **14.** $\frac{13}{16}$

15. $101\frac{9}{16}$ **16.** $\frac{7}{8}$ **17.** $27\frac{1}{4}$ **18.** $\frac{7}{16}$

19. $3\frac{13}{16}$ **20.** $22\frac{7}{8}$ **21.** $43\frac{1}{16}$ **22.** $90\frac{3}{4}$

23. $\frac{3}{8}$ **24.** $9\frac{11}{16}$ **25.** $\frac{3}{4}$ **26.** $8\frac{5}{16}$

27. $\frac{15}{16}$ **28.** $\frac{5}{8}$ **29.** $\frac{9}{16}$ **30.** $7\frac{7}{16}$

DECIMALS

page 2

WORKED EXAMPLE

$12\frac{3}{8} = 12$ and $\frac{3}{8}$

$= 12$ and 0.375

$= 12.375$

$8\overline{)3.000}$ $\quad 0.375$

Write each mixed number, whole number, or fraction as a decimal. Carry to four decimal places if necessary. Do not round answers.

1. $1\frac{1}{8}$ **2.** $\frac{1}{4}$

3. $17\frac{1}{16}$ **4.** $16\frac{3}{4}$ **5.** $\frac{11}{16}$ **6.** $7\frac{1}{2}$

7. $6\frac{13}{16}$ **8.** $26\frac{7}{8}$ **9.** $\frac{15}{16}$ **10.** $25\frac{1}{16}$

11. $30\frac{1}{8}$ **12.** $2\frac{5}{8}$ **13.** $29\frac{7}{16}$ **14.** $\frac{3}{16}$

15. $3\frac{1}{2}$ **16.** 12 **17.** $19\frac{7}{16}$ **18.** 15

19. $13\frac{15}{16}$ **20.** $18\frac{3}{16}$ **21.** $4\frac{3}{8}$ **22.** 28

23. $8\frac{5}{8}$ **24.** $22\frac{5}{16}$ **25.** $21\frac{9}{16}$ **26.** $20\frac{7}{8}$

27. $3\frac{1}{4}$ **28.** $9\frac{3}{8}$ **29.** $27\frac{1}{2}$ **30.** $14\frac{1}{8}$

ANSWERS

1. 1.125
2. 0.25
3. 17.0625
4. 16.75
5. 0.6875
6. 7.5
7. 6.8125
8. 26.875
9. 0.9375
10. 25.0625
11. 30.125
12. 2.625
13. 29.4375
14. 0.1875
15. 3.5
16. 12.0
17. 19.4375
18. 15.0
19. 13.9375
20. 18.1875
21. 4.375
22. 28.0
23. 8.625
24. 22.3125
25. 21.5625
26. 20.875
27. 3.25
28. 9.375
29. 27.5
30. 14.125

ANSWERS

1. 16.333
2. 8.056
3. 10.133
4. 22.222
5. 7.067
6. 28.111
7. 29.083
8. 3.611
9. 11.944
10. 17.933
11. 6.667
12. 12.389
13. 21.033
14. 27.722
15. 15.417
16. 26.467
17. 2.889
18. 20.533
19. 25.278
20. 1.444
21. 13.917
22. 30.433
23. 4.267
24. 14.733
25. 24.233
26. 19.778
27. 9.583
28. 18.367
29. 5.556
30. 23.867

WORKED EXAMPLE

$11\frac{5}{6} = 11$ and $\frac{5}{6}$

$= 11$ and 0.833

$= 11.833$

$6)\overline{5.0000}$ 0.8333 $\doteq 0.833$

Write each mixed number as a decimal. Round to the nearest thousandth.

1. $16\frac{1}{3}$
2. $8\frac{1}{18}$
3. $10\frac{2}{15}$
4. $22\frac{2}{9}$
5. $7\frac{1}{15}$
6. $28\frac{1}{9}$
7. $29\frac{1}{12}$
8. $3\frac{11}{18}$
9. $11\frac{17}{18}$
10. $17\frac{14}{15}$
11. $6\frac{2}{3}$
12. $12\frac{7}{18}$
13. $21\frac{1}{30}$
14. $27\frac{13}{18}$
15. $15\frac{5}{12}$
16. $26\frac{7}{15}$
17. $2\frac{8}{9}$
18. $20\frac{8}{15}$
19. $25\frac{5}{18}$
20. $1\frac{4}{9}$
21. $13\frac{11}{12}$
22. $30\frac{13}{30}$
23. $4\frac{4}{15}$
24. $14\frac{11}{15}$
25. $24\frac{7}{30}$
26. $19\frac{7}{9}$
27. $9\frac{7}{12}$
28. $18\frac{11}{30}$
29. $5\frac{5}{9}$
30. $23\frac{13}{15}$

410

OBJECTIVE   Skill 4   Write decimals as fractions and mixed numbers.

SKILL MODEL

PROBLEM	1	2	3	ANSWER
Write 0.0125 as a fraction.	THINK 0.0125 is 125 ten-thousandths	125 ten-thousandths = $\dfrac{125}{10,000}$	$\dfrac{125}{10,000} = \dfrac{1}{80}$	$0.0125 = \dfrac{1}{80}$

SOLUTION STEPS

Step 1   Think of the place-value name of the decimal.

Step 2   Write the place-value name as a fraction.

Step 3   Write the fraction in lowest terms.

Step 4   Write the answer.

> **NOTE**
>
> $0.0125 = \dfrac{125}{10,000}$
>
> 4 decimal places   4 zeros

> **NOTE**
>
> If a decimal number has a whole number part, write the decimal part as a fraction and add the whole number part.
>
> $4.17 = 4 + 0.17 = 4 + \dfrac{17}{100} = 4\dfrac{17}{100}$

WORKED EXAMPLES

1. $0.04 = \dfrac{4}{100} = \dfrac{1}{25}$

2. $2.75 = 2\dfrac{75}{100} = 2\dfrac{3}{4}$

3. $9.003 = 9\dfrac{3}{1000}$

BRUSH-UP EXERCISES

Write each decimal as a fraction or mixed number.

1. 4.5

2. 12.6

3. 124.2

4. 6.15

5. 17.45

6. 364.64

7. 16.50

8. 0.32

9. 164.75

10. 9.004

11. 0.065

12. 450.4

SELF-CHECK ANSWERS

1. $4\dfrac{1}{2}$ 2. $12\dfrac{3}{5}$ 3. $124\dfrac{1}{5}$ 4. $6\dfrac{3}{20}$ 5. $17\dfrac{9}{20}$ 6. $364\dfrac{16}{25}$ 7. $16\dfrac{1}{2}$

8. $\dfrac{8}{25}$ 9. $164\dfrac{3}{4}$ 10. $9\dfrac{1}{250}$ 11. $\dfrac{13}{200}$ 12. $450\dfrac{2}{5}$

PRACTICE   DECIMALS   Skill 4

1. $\frac{4}{5}$
2. $7\frac{1}{10}$
3. $2\frac{2}{5}$
4. $\frac{3}{10}$
5. $7\frac{1}{2}$
6. $7\frac{3}{5}$
7. $6\frac{1}{5}$
8. $\frac{6}{25}$
9. $8\frac{9}{20}$
10. $1\frac{31}{50}$
11. $4\frac{8}{25}$
12. $7\frac{1}{2}$
13. $\frac{9}{25}$
14. $5\frac{12}{25}$
15. $9\frac{1}{10}$
16. $8\frac{1}{2}$
17. $7\frac{3}{20}$
18. $9\frac{3}{10}$
19. $\frac{1}{50}$
20. $9\frac{1}{20}$
21. 8
22. $7\frac{1}{25}$
23. $40\frac{1}{4}$
24. $16\frac{11}{20}$
25. $28\frac{4}{25}$
26. $\frac{21}{50}$
27. $140\frac{18}{25}$
28. 624
29. $236\frac{9}{25}$
30. $442\frac{16}{25}$
31. $571\frac{7}{20}$

WORKED EXAMPLE

$2.2 = 2\frac{2}{10} = 2\frac{1}{5}$

Write each decimal as a mixed number or whole number or fraction. Reduce to lowest terms.

1. $0.8 = $ _____

2. $7.1 = $ _____
3. $2.4 = $ _____
4. $0.3 = $ _____

5. $7.5 = $ _____
6. $7.6 = $ _____
7. $6.20 = $ _____

8. $0.24 = $ _____
9. $8.45 = $ _____
10. $1.62 = $ _____

11. $4.32 = $ _____
12. $7.50 = $ _____
13. $0.36 = $ _____

14. $5.48 = $ _____
15. $9.10 = $ _____
16. $8.500 = $ _____

17. $7.15 = $ _____
18. $9.30 = $ _____
19. $0.02 = $ _____

20. $9.05 = $ _____
21. $8.00 = $ _____
22. $7.04 = $ _____

23. $40.25 = $ _____
24. $16.55 = $ _____
25. $28.16 = $ _____

26. $0.42 = $ _____
27. $140.72 = $ _____
28. $624.00 = $ _____

29. $236.36 = $ _____
30. $442.64 = $ _____
31. $571.35 = $ _____

Copyright © 1980 by Houghton Mifflin Company. All rights reserved.

WORKED EXAMPLE

$$7.165 = 7\frac{165}{1000} = 7\frac{33}{200}$$

Write each decimal as a mixed number. Reduce to lowest terms.

1. $4.040 =$ _____

2. $6.032 =$ _____

3. $7.700 =$ _____

4. $9.900 =$ _____

5. $6.060 =$ _____

6. $3.048 =$ _____

7. $4.650 =$ _____

8. $6.808 =$ _____

9. $8.202 =$ _____

10. $9.648 =$ _____

11. $16.004 =$ _____

12. $14.008 =$ _____

13. $18.020 =$ _____

14. $12.080 =$ _____

15. $38.211 =$ _____

16. $42.666 =$ _____

17. $63.428 =$ _____

18. $41.364 =$ _____

19. $34.448 =$ _____

20. $60.256 =$ _____

21. $35.333 =$ _____

22. $40.107 =$ _____

23. $63.060 =$ _____

24. $47.248 =$ _____

25. $67.425 =$ _____

26. $90.328 =$ _____

27. $123.450 =$ _____

28. $345.080 =$ _____

29. $456.005 =$ _____

30. $128.036 =$ _____

31. $243.002 =$ _____

ANSWERS

1. $4\frac{1}{25}$
2. $6\frac{4}{125}$
3. $7\frac{7}{10}$
4. $9\frac{9}{10}$
5. $6\frac{3}{50}$
6. $3\frac{6}{125}$
7. $4\frac{13}{20}$
8. $6\frac{101}{125}$
9. $8\frac{101}{500}$
10. $9\frac{81}{125}$
11. $16\frac{1}{250}$
12. $14\frac{1}{125}$
13. $18\frac{1}{50}$
14. $12\frac{2}{25}$
15. $38\frac{211}{1000}$
16. $42\frac{333}{500}$
17. $63\frac{107}{250}$
18. $41\frac{91}{250}$
19. $34\frac{56}{125}$
20. $60\frac{32}{125}$
21. $35\frac{333}{1000}$
22. $40\frac{107}{1000}$
23. $63\frac{3}{50}$
24. $47\frac{31}{125}$
25. $67\frac{17}{40}$
26. $90\frac{41}{125}$
27. $123\frac{9}{20}$
28. $345\frac{2}{25}$
29. $456\frac{1}{200}$
30. $128\frac{9}{250}$
31. $243\frac{1}{500}$

SKILL 1

1. 2.7
2. 137.003
3. 10.025
4. 56.102
5. 5.0080
6. 0.017

SKILL 1   Write as decimals.

1. 2 and 7 tenths
2. 137 and 3 thousandths
3. 10 and 25 thousandths
4. 56 and 102 thousandths
5. Five and eighty ten-thousandths
6. Seventeen thousandths

SKILL 2

1. 19.3
2. 27.8
3. 3.06
4. 135.72
5. 16.890
6. 0.1070

SKILL 2

1. Round 19.347 to the nearest tenth.
2. Round 27.750 to the nearest tenth.
3. Round 3.057 to the nearest hundredth.
4. Round 135.721 to the nearest hundredth.
5. Round 16.8897 to the nearest thousandth.
6. Round 0.10702 to the nearest ten-thousandth.

SKILL 3

1. 8.13
2. 2.75
3. 6.667
4. 0.889
5. 1.083
6. 5.438

SKILL 3   Write as decimals. If necessary, round to the nearest thousandth.

1. $8\frac{13}{100}$
2. $2\frac{3}{4}$
3. $6\frac{2}{3}$
4. $\frac{8}{9}$
5. $1\frac{1}{12}$
6. $5\frac{7}{16}$

SKILL 4

1. $\frac{3}{10}$
2. $2\frac{17}{100}$
3. $121\frac{7}{20}$
4. $8\frac{12}{25}$
5. $17\frac{1}{8}$
6. $3\frac{24}{125}$

SKILL 4   Write as fractions or mixed numbers in lowest terms.

1. 0.3
2. 2.17
3. 121.35
4. 8.48
5. 17.125
6. 3.192

OBJECTIVE   Skill 5   Add decimals to ten-thousandths
with no regrouping.

SKILL MODEL

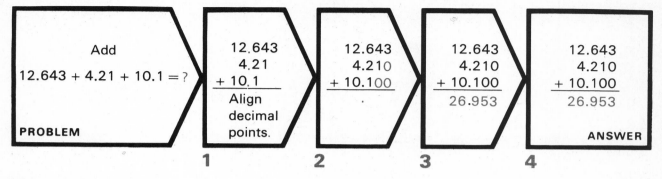

SOLUTION STEPS

Step 1   Write the addition problem in
vertical form, aligning decimal
points.

Step 2   Write a zero in each blank decimal
place. Then, write a decimal point
directly below the decimal points
in the problem.

Step 3   Add.

Step 4   Write the answer.

WORKED EXAMPLES

1.
```
   $41.21
 +   6.76
   $47.97
```

2.
```
   104.0025
    11.15
 +   4.637
   119.7895
```

3. 9.43 + 30.2
```
      9.43
 +  30.2
    39.63
```

BRUSH-UP EXERCISES

1.
```
   $24.21
 +   3.65
```

2.
```
   $127.12
 +   31.43
```

3.
```
    402.07
     23.104
 + 142.315
```

4.
```
   126.4116
    30.025
 + 112.32
```

5. 126.041 + 11.42 + 230.116

6. 42.216 + 100.06 + 623.5221

SELF-CHECK ANSWERS

1. $27.86   2. $158.55   3. 567.489   4. 268.7566   5. 367.577   6. 765.7981

Add.

1. $0.13
+ 0.80

2. $0.40
+ 0.21

3. $ 4.32
+ 21.04

4. $ 14.41
+ 102.36

5. $0.41
0.20
+ 0.33

6. $0.01
0.26
+ 0.12

7. $124.34
11.20
+ 4.10

8. $ 14.40
102.13
+ 61.24

9. $202.21
136.42
+ 150.13

10. $102.40
321.37
+ 464.11

11. $226.62
101.16
+ 142.01

12. $124.05
232.12
+ 403.60

13. $301.41
247.10
+ 120.02

14. $312.12
116.14
+ 401.21

15. $112.21
404.13
+ 413.45

16. $414.01
342.22
+ 121.06

Rewrite each problem in vertical form, then add.

17. $0.26 + $0.02

18. $13.42 + $212.16

19. $0.13 + $0.21 + $6.14

20. $19.20 + $10.43 + $200.10

21. $201.05 + $141.21 + $435.63

22. $142.35 + $213.11 + $402.12

PRACTICE   DECIMALS   Skill 5

WORKED EXAMPLE
8.24
+ 30.412
38.652

Add.

1.   0.6
    + 0.24

2.   0.37
    + 0.12

3.   22.4
    + 3.28

4.   18.02
    + 4.23

5.   23.4
    + 2.06

6.   6.01
    + 21.36

7.   9.42
    + 20.213

8.   0.21
    + 49.101

9.   18.434
    + 0.21

10.   22.001
    + 3.01

11.   102.0241
    + 16.101

12.   120.081
    + 46.4023

13.   106.435
    + 221.242

14.   103.210
    + 400.0361

Rewrite each problem in vertical form, then add.

15. 0.24 + 0.6217

16. 0.43 + 0.142

17. 7.36 + 12.2175

18. 24.062 + 11.424

19. 103.405 + 85.37

20. 164.205 + 420.5835

417

Add.

1. 0.2
  + 0.167

2. 4.31
  + 2.4662

3. 7.0021
  + 2.01

4. 6.423
  + 2.0463

5. 3.04
  + 12.113

6. 26.63
  + 32.1447

7. 127.213
  + 11.0145

8. 213.416
  + 104.3421

9. 0.41
    0.2024
  + 0.016

10. 24.001
     3.01
  + 101.01

11. 20.21
    112.034
  + 46.012

12. 412.4
    102.063
  + 315.21

13. 14.203
     2.0046
  + 132.16

14. 12.4
    42.213
  + 204.1661

15. 123.215
    224.1218
  + 131.2

16. 120.04
    243.6
  + 304.2041

Rewrite each problem in vertical form, then add.

17. 8.7 + 1.025

18. 3.64 + 4.2454

19. 12.41 + 136.2432

20. 742.241 + 106.3572

21. 7.307 + 281.1 + 400.1916

22. 205.141 + 33.42 + 1.0183

LESSON   DECIMALS   Skill 6

OBJECTIVE   Skill 6   Add decimals to ten-thousandths with regrouping.

SKILL MODEL

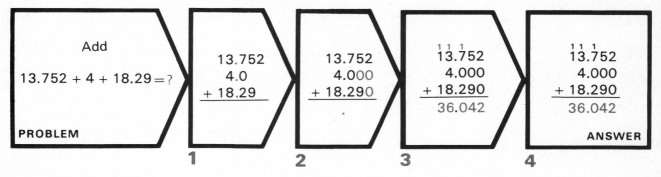

SOLUTION STEPS

Step 1   Write the addition problem in vertical form, aligning decimal points.

Step 2   Write a zero in each blank decimal place. Then write a decimal point directly below the decimal points in the problem.

Step 3   Add. Regroup as necessary.

Step 4   Write the answer.

WORKED EXAMPLES

1.
$$\begin{array}{r} \overset{1\ 1\ 1}{\$\ 76.46} \\ +\ \ 139.86 \\ \hline \$216.32 \end{array}$$

2.
$$\begin{array}{r} \overset{1\ \ 1}{9.83} \\ +\ 30.2 \\ \hline 40.03 \end{array}$$

3. 167.889 + 36 + 63.24
$$\begin{array}{r} \overset{1\ 1\ 1\ \ 1}{167.889} \\ 36 \\ +\ \ 63.24 \\ \hline 267.129 \end{array}$$

BRUSH-UP EXERCISES

1.
$$\begin{array}{r} \$609.72 \\ +\ \ \ 19.29 \\ \hline \end{array}$$

2.
$$\begin{array}{r} \$1508.33 \\ +\ \ \ \ 601.67 \\ \hline \end{array}$$

3.
$$\begin{array}{r} 37.27 \\ +\ 184.948 \\ \hline \end{array}$$

4.
$$\begin{array}{r} 124.63 \\ 87.272 \\ +\ \ \ 0.091 \\ \hline \end{array}$$

5. 24.697 + 8.1041

6. 76.1073 + 3.723 + 265.4829

SELF-CHECK ANSWERS

1. $629.01   2. $2110.00   3. 222.218   4. 211.993   5. 32.8011   6. 345.3132

ANSWERS

1. $0.71
2. $1.25
3. $1.02
4. $1.12
5. $43.71
6. $122.38
7. $514.25
8. $1162.21
9. $1.72
10. $1.35
11. $1.26
12. $1.64
13. $239.18
14. $210.62
15. $375.55
16. $1042.62
17. $1.70
18. $32.60
19. $7.38
20. $3.08
21. $1474.28
22. $1355.94

Add.

1. $0.67
+ 0.04

2. $0.35
+ 0.90

3. $0.60
+ 0.42

4. $0.74
+ 0.38

5. $ 7.68
+ 36.03

6. $42.90
+ 79.48

7. $ 86.86
+ 427.39

8. $697.35
+ 464.86

9. $0.68
0.70
+ 0.34

10. $0.06
0.82
+ 0.47

11. $0.29
0.62
+ 0.35

12. $0.25
0.43
+ 0.96

13. $ 4.67
38.09
+ 196.42

14. $ 24.47
176.80
+ 9.35

15. $ 36.70
273.26
+ 65.59

16. $ 22.65
76.37
+ 943.60

Rewrite each problem in vertical form, then add.

17. $0.74 + $0.96

18. $7.64 + $24.96

19. $0.76 + $5.07 + $1.55

20. $0.80 + $0.64 + $1.64

21. $476.73 + $135.46 + $862.09

22. $183.52 + $423.68 + $748.74

PRACTICE

DECIMALS

WORKED EXAMPLE

$$
\begin{array}{r}
416.788 \\
+\ 97.93 \\
\hline
514.718
\end{array}
$$

Add.

1.
$$
\begin{array}{r}
0.494 \\
+\ 0.83 \\
\hline
\end{array}
$$

2.
$$
\begin{array}{r}
0.65 \\
+\ 0.796 \\
\hline
\end{array}
$$

3.
$$
\begin{array}{r}
124.235 \\
+\ 83.97 \\
\hline
\end{array}
$$

4.
$$
\begin{array}{r}
76.78 \\
+\ 438.946 \\
\hline
\end{array}
$$

5.
$$
\begin{array}{r}
169.278 \\
+\ 46.96 \\
\hline
\end{array}
$$

6.
$$
\begin{array}{r}
943.94 \\
+\ 68.289 \\
\hline
\end{array}
$$

7.
$$
\begin{array}{r}
496.008 \\
+\ 568.0039 \\
\hline
\end{array}
$$

8.
$$
\begin{array}{r}
947.04 \\
+\ 365.074 \\
\hline
\end{array}
$$

9.
$$
\begin{array}{r}
600.903 \\
+\ 800.5097 \\
\hline
\end{array}
$$

10.
$$
\begin{array}{r}
80.629 \\
+\ 649.5 \\
\hline
\end{array}
$$

11.
$$
\begin{array}{r}
814.08 \\
+\ 399.0496 \\
\hline
\end{array}
$$

12.
$$
\begin{array}{r}
206.047 \\
+\ 395 \\
\hline
\end{array}
$$

13.
$$
\begin{array}{r}
965.07 \\
+\ 776.0951 \\
\hline
\end{array}
$$

14.
$$
\begin{array}{r}
641.279 \\
+\ 359.7 \\
\hline
\end{array}
$$

Rewrite each problem in vertical form, then add.

15. $0.469 + 0.5876$

16. $275.48 + 79.377$

17. $36.84 + 874.9072$

18. $897.741 + 68.2911$

19. $714.529 + 297.6769$

20. $383.406 + 578.7948$

ANSWERS

1. 1.324
2. 1.446
3. 208.205
4. 515.726
5. 216.238
6. 1012.229
7. 1064.0119
8. 1312.114
9. 1401.4127
10. 730.129
11. 1213.1296
12. 601.047
13. 1741.1651
14. 1000.979
15. 1.0566
16. 354.857
17. 911.7472
18. 966.0321
19. 1012.2059
20. 962.2008

421

Add.

1.
```
   8.3
   5.853
+ 2.87
```

2.
```
   5.84
   0.9717
+ 7.13
```

3.
```
   7.83
   3.976
+ 3.44
```

4.
```
   7.88
   3.9248
+ 8.116
```

5.
```
   8.267
  38.17
+ 95.896
```

6.
```
  285.36
   75.0091
+ 315.9
```

7.
```
  792.6
   34.18
+  78.09
```

8.
```
  8267.85
   115.7
+  741.48
```

9.
```
  301.02
  872
+  36.9748
```

10.
```
  412.547
    8.4
+  75.8364
```

11.
```
  400.212
  286.7386
+  67.849
```

12.
```
  472.9
  684.712
+836
```

13.
```
  474.67
   49.4361
+   7.4
```

14.
```
  637.04
  193.764
+   8.40
```

15.
```
    9.461
   27.3478
+ 691.9
```

16.
```
  426.94
   37.4087
+ 867.27
```

Rewrite each problem in vertical form, then add.

17. $8.467 + 9.84 + 0.8763$

18. $6.27 + 0.429 + 9.4$

19. $147.689 + 4 + 3.0045$

20. $965.97 + 72 + 3.701$

21. $42.707 + 815 + 32.06$

22. $485.557 + 13.69 + 300$

OBJECTIVE   Skill 7   Subtract decimals to ten-thousandths with no regrouping.

SKILL MODEL

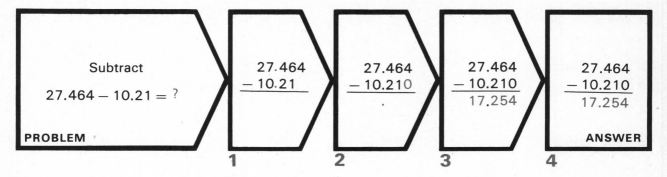

SOLUTION STEPS

Step 1   Write the subtraction problem in vertical form, aligning decimal points.

Step 2   Write a zero in each blank decimal place. Then write a decimal point directly below the decimal points in the problem.

Step 3   Subtract.

Step 4   Write the answer.

WORKED EXAMPLES

1.
$$\begin{array}{r} \$39.59 \\ -\ 3.21 \\ \hline \$36.38 \end{array}$$

2.
$$\begin{array}{r} 784.534 \\ -\ 501.2 \\ \hline 283.334 \end{array}$$

3. 54.137 − 12.02
$$\begin{array}{r} 54.137 \\ -\ 12.02 \\ \hline 42.117 \end{array}$$

BRUSH-UP EXERCISES

1.
$$\begin{array}{r} \$28.64 \\ -\ 13.21 \\ \hline \end{array}$$

2.
$$\begin{array}{r} \$463.27 \\ -\ 41.16 \\ \hline \end{array}$$

3.
$$\begin{array}{r} 879.4138 \\ -\ 160.212 \\ \hline \end{array}$$

4.
$$\begin{array}{r} 762.381 \\ -\ 40.25 \\ \hline \end{array}$$

5. 47.632 − 5.41

6. 637.4568 − 125.234

SELF-CHECK ANSWERS

1. $15.43   2. $422.11   3. 719.2018   4. 722.131   5. 42.222   6. 512.2228

ANSWERS
1. $0.37
2. $0.21
3. $0.50
4. $0.12
5. $4.12
6. $4.72
7. $1.14
8. $1.01
9. $22.23
10. $121.81
11. $110.20
12. $222.31
13. $320.14
14. $322.01
15. $3.30
16. $0
17. $2.37
18. $2.22
19. $21.11
20. $45.11
21. $100.03
22. $254.32

Subtract.

1. $0.97
      − 0.60

2. $0.48
      − 0.27

3. $0.56
      − 0.06

4. $0.86
      − 0.74

5. $8.82
      − 4.70

6. $7.75
      − 3.03

7. $2.27
      − 1.13

8. $7.06
      − 6.05

9. $24.39
      −   2.16

10. $127.82
       −   6.01

11. $143.24
       −   33.04

12. $292.79
       −   70.48

13. $465.28
       − 145.14

14. $496.12
       − 174.11

15. $233.35
       − 230.05

16. $764.82
       − 764.82

Rewrite each problem in vertical form, then subtract.

17. $4.67 − $2.30

18. $8.43 − $6.21

19. $24.93 − $3.82

20. $69.46 − $24.35

21. $126.49 − $26.46

22. $378.65 − $124.33

PRACTICE

DECIMALS

Skill 7

WORKED EXAMPLE
6.38   − 0.14   6.24

Subtract.

1.   0.46
 − 0.2

2.   0.38
 − 0.1

3.   6.72
 − 2.21

4.   3.48
 − 0.24

5.   4.20
 − 2.10

6.   6.27
 − 4.14

7.   28.34
 − 4.03

8.   83.72
 − 1.21

9.   72.16
 − 60.12

10.   49.20
 − 24.10

11.   263.46
 − 22.24

12.   134.27
 − 12.07

13.   289.47
 − 147.07

14.   675.84
 − 475.60

Rewrite each problem in vertical form, then subtract.

15. 4.81 − 2.3

16. 7.34 − 4.1

17. 27.28 − 11.03

18. 42.63 − 20.41

19. 146.243 − 13.13

20. 497.729 − 364.527

ANSWERS
1. 0.26
2. 0.28
3. 4.51
4. 3.24
5. 2.1
6. 2.13
7. 24.31
8. 82.51
9. 12.04
10. 25.1
11. 241.22
12. 122.2
13. 142.4
14. 200.24
15. 2.51
16. 3.24
17. 16.25
18. 22.22
19. 133.113
20. 133.202

425

ANSWERS
1. 0.574
2. 0.126
3. 3.129
4. 1.036
5. 4.3233
6. 6.2222
7. 72.219
8. 111.128
9. 310.006
10. 92.026
11. 332.0905
12. 211.1308
13. 310.1011
14. 110.2422
15. 2.063
16. 14.633
17. 110.1451
18. 314.1048
19. 206.2222
20. 541.21

WORKED EXAMPLE

$$387.297 - 47.17 = \begin{array}{r} 387.297 \\ -\ \ 47.17 \\ \hline 340.127 \end{array}$$

Subtract.

1. 0.974
    − 0.4

2. 0.286
    − 0.16

3. 7.729
    − 4.6

4. 9.276
    − 8.24

5. 6.4273
    − 2.104

6. 6.3272
    − 0.105

7. 74.569
    − 2.35

8. 129.838
    − 18.71

9. 478.926
    − 168.92

10. 92.146
    − 0.12

11. 334.2945
    − 2.204

12. 263.3618
    − 52.231

13. 464.2071
    − 154.106

14. 830.4672
    − 720.225

Rewrite each problem in vertical form, then subtract.

15. 7.463 − 5.4

16. 28.863 − 14.23

17. 124.2751 − 14.13

18. 374.8048 − 60.70

19. 326.4852 − 120.263

20. 865.216 − 324.006

LESSON   DECIMALS   Skill 8

OBJECTIVE   Skill 8   Subtract decimals to ten-thousandths
                            with regrouping.

SKILL MODEL

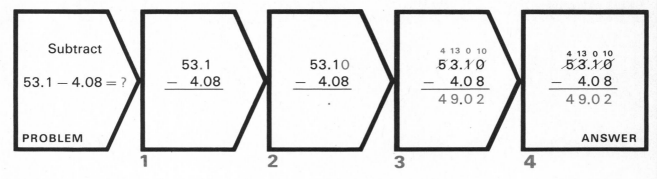

SOLUTION STEPS

Step 1 Write the subtraction problem in vertical form, aligning decimal points.

Step 2 Write a zero in each blank decimal place. Then write a decimal point directly below the decimal points in the problem.

Step 3 Subtract. Regroup and borrow as necessary.

Step 4 Write the answer.

WORKED EXAMPLES

1. $15.87
   −   9.93
   $ 5.94

2. 118.50
   −   6.73
   111.77

3. 807 − 19.302

   807.000
   − 19.302
   787.698

BRUSH-UP EXERCISES

1. $6.00
   − 2.58

2. $20.75
   − 5.98

3. 129.6
   − 18.77

4. 2000.38
   −   57.99

5. 231.1 − 9.837

6. 500 − 0.0028

SELF-CHECK ANSWERS

1. $3.42   2. $14.77   3. 110.83   4. 1942.39   5. 221.263   6. 499.9972

427

ANSWERS

1. $0.58
2. $0.29
3. $0.07
4. $0.15
5. $1.82
6. $3.47
7. $87.89
8. $61.68
9. $115.69
10. $278.88
11. $429.18
12. $778.19
13. $198.09
14. $198.86
15. $178.38
16. $89.09
17. $0.59
18. $0.97
19. $67.75
20. $24.85
21. $78.59
22. $178.97

Subtract.

1. $0.67
    − 0.09

2. $0.38
    − 0.09

3. $0.41
    − 0.34

4. $0.84
    − 0.69

5. $8.67
    − 6.85

6. $6.21
    − 2.74

7. $96.47
    − 8.58

8. $62.37
    − 0.69

9. $123.12
    − 7.43

10. $286.34
    − 7.46

11. $448.27
    − 19.09

12. $864.28
    − 86.09

13. $446.07
    − 247.98

14. $378.70
    − 179.84

15. $374.02
    − 195.64

16. $278.05
    − 188.96

Rewrite each problem in vertical form, then subtract.

17. $0.68 − $0.09

18. $6.43 − $5.46

19. $68.31 − $0.56

20. $73.50 − $48.65

21. $126.43 − $47.84

22. $460.35 − $281.38

<table>
<tr><td colspan="3" align="center">**WORKED EXAMPLE**</td></tr>
<tr><td colspan="3" align="center">9.4
− 0.94
8.46</td></tr>
</table>

Subtract.

1.   4.6
     − 0.8

2.   8.3
     − 4.5

3.   9.63
     − 4.7

4.   6.02
     − 3.4

5.   18.46
     − 9.9

6.   23.84
     − 6.9

7.   36.437
     − 6.94

8.   68.203
     − 29.4

9.   321.3
     − 77.85

10.   386.553
     − 97.88

11.   32.861
     − 25.87

12.   483.4
     − 94.687

13.   286.7
     − 283.099

14.   276
     − 178.948

Rewrite each problem in vertical form, then subtract.

15. 6.34 − 0.6

16. 6.73 − 2.7

17. 49 − 27.94

18. 129.6 − 19.79

19. 673.3 − 274.333

20. 270.4 − 184.663

ANSWERS
1. 3.8
2. 3.8
3. 4.93
4. 2.62
5. 8.56
6. 16.94
7. 29.497
8. 38.803
9. 243.45
10. 288.673
11. 6.991
12. 388.713
13. 3.601
14. 97.052
15. 5.74
16. 4.03
17. 21.06
18. 109.81
19. 398.967
20. 85.737

ANSWERS
1. 5.44
2. 3.06
3. 8.93
4. 28.94
5. 108.674
6. 335.697
7. 8.771
8. 169.755
9. 99.673
10. 289.317
11. 170.427
12. 397.901
13. 104.194
14. 9.79
15. 14.06
16. 26.18
17. 49.528
18. 187.306
19. 340.784
20. 87.796

WORKED EXAMPLE

$$\begin{array}{r} 1\,4\,6 \\ -\ \ 8\,6.4\,5\,8 \\ \hline 5\,9.5\,4\,2 \end{array}$$

Subtract.

1. 6.2
    − 0.76

2. 7
    − 3.94

3. 14.6
    − 5.67

4. 47.8
    − 18.86

5. 126.434
    − 17.76

6. 464.517
    − 128.82

7. 28.41
    − 19.639

8. 437.1
    − 267.345

9. 268.62
    − 168.947

10. 463.407
    − 174.09

11. 200.1
    − 29.673

12. 472.4
    − 74.499

13. 268.41
    − 164.216

14. 162.2
    − 152.41

Rewrite each problem in vertical form, then subtract.

15. 23.4 − 9.34

16. 64 − 37.82

17. 147 − 97.472

18. 382 − 194.694

19. 427.21 − 86.426

20. 274 − 186.204

WORKED EXAMPLE
4228.94 − 194.08 4034.86

Subtract.

1. 10.24
− 0.618

2. 20.135
− 0.466

3. 28.8
− 7.94

4. 48.74
− 46.9

5. 68.08
− 43.96

6. 72.37
− 49.84

7. 126.6
− 9.874

8. 147.431
− 138.9

9. 264.678
− 186.84

10. 193.955
− 148.68

11. 1426.69
− 785.5456

12. 5365.91
− 482.09

13. 634.06
− 480.9

14. 708.97
− 497.031

Rewrite each problem in vertical form, then subtract.

15. 0.91 − 0.489

16. 10.42 − 0.687

17. 98.6 − 97.84

18. 143.69 − 78.35

19. 769.85 − 403.1732

20. 672.875 − 499.2664

ANSWERS

1. 9.622
2. 19.669
3. 20.86
4. 1.84
5. 24.12
6. 22.53
7. 116.726
8. 8.531
9. 77.838
10. 45.275
11. 641.1444
12. 4883.82
13. 153.16
14. 211.939
15. 0.421
16. 9.733
17. 0.76
18. 65.34
19. 366.6768
20. 173.6086

431

SKILL 5
1. $18.75
2. 19.951
3. $179.79
4. 68.349
5. 19.55
6. 89.998

SKILL 6
1. 12.62
2. $31.48
3. 162.765
4. 26.196
5. 120.31
6. 2.2137

SKILL 7
1. $12.33
2. 14.45
3. 27.1215
4. 221.2022
5. 103.3
6. 0.018

SKILL 8
1. $7.81
2. 118.92
3. 1.9295
4. $8.01
5. 5.6301
6. 0.036

SKILL 5
1. $13.50 + 5.25
2. 9.2 + 10.751
3. $165.39 + 14.40
4. 62.331 + 5.01 + 1.008
5. 2.35 + 17.2
6. 88.01 + 1.988

SKILL 6
1. 6.81 + 5.81
2. $16.50 + 14.98
3. 145.37 + 17.395
4. 8.009 + 17.31 + 0.877
5. 5.6 + 114.71
6. 0.0167 + 2.197

SKILL 7
1. $15.95 − 3.62
2. 18.75 − 4.3
3. 29.1385 − 2.017
4. 781.3072 − 560.105
5. 108.3 − 5
6. 0.048 − 0.03

SKILL 8
1. $57.39 − 49.58
2. 126.82 − 7.9
3. 3.0015 − 1.072
4. $15.00 − 6.99
5. 8.7201 − 3.09
6. 0.125 − 0.089

OBJECTIVE   Skill 9   Multiply a decimal by a whole number.

SKILL MODEL

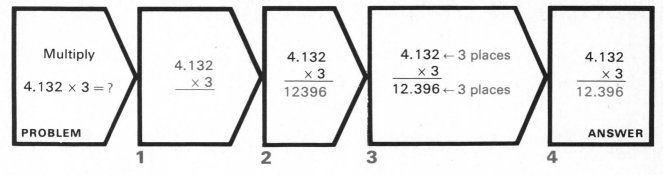

PROBLEM	1	2	3	4 ANSWER
Multiply $4.132 \times 3 = ?$	$\begin{array}{r} 4.132 \\ \times\ 3 \\ \hline \end{array}$	$\begin{array}{r} 4.132 \\ \times\ 3 \\ \hline 12396 \end{array}$	$\begin{array}{r} 4.132 \leftarrow 3\ places \\ \times\ 3 \\ \hline 12.396 \leftarrow 3\ places \end{array}$	$\begin{array}{r} 4.132 \\ \times\ 3 \\ \hline 12.396 \end{array}$

SOLUTION STEPS

Step 1   Write the multiplication problem in vertical form with the decimal in the top line.

Step 2   Multiply as if the decimal number were a whole number.

Step 3   Count the number of decimal places in the decimal. Write a decimal point in the answer so that the answer has the same number of decimal places.

Step 4   Write the answer.

UNDERSTAND

$$\begin{array}{l} 4.132 \\ \underline{\times\ 3} \\ 0.006 \leftarrow 3 \times 2\ thousandths \\ 0.09 \leftarrow 3 \times 3\ hundredths \\ 0.3 \leftarrow 3 \times 1\ tenth \\ \underline{12} \leftarrow 3 \times 4\ ones \\ 12.396 \end{array}$$

WORKED EXAMPLES

1. $\begin{array}{r} \$3.05 \\ \times\ 9 \\ \hline \$27.45 \end{array}$

2. $\begin{array}{r} 118.173 \\ \times\ 148 \\ \hline 945\ 484 \\ 4\ 926\ 92 \\ 11\ 817\ 3 \\ \hline 17,489.604 \end{array}$

3. 16.18×25

$\begin{array}{r} 16.18 \\ \times\ 25 \\ \hline 80\ 90 \\ 323\ 6 \\ \hline 404.50 \end{array}$

BRUSH-UP EXERCISES

1. $\begin{array}{r} 4.28 \\ \times\ 6 \\ \hline \end{array}$

2. $\begin{array}{r} 82.14 \\ \times\ 32 \\ \hline \end{array}$

3. $\begin{array}{r} 67.43 \\ \times\ 212 \\ \hline \end{array}$

4. $\begin{array}{r} 325.87 \\ \times\ 436 \\ \hline \end{array}$

5. 1.05×700

6. 256×6.07

SELF-CHECK ANSWERS

1. 25.68   **2.** 2628.48   **3.** 14,295.16   **4.** 142,079.32   **5.** 735   **6.** 1553.92

ANSWERS
1. 0.02
2. 10.02
3. 30
4. 3
5. 0.3
6. 100.3
7. 80
8. 8
9. 0.8
10. 200.8
11. 150
12. 15
13. 1.5
14. 301.5
15. 0.6
16. 10.06
17. 35
18. 503.5
19. 48
20. 604.8

WORKED EXAMPLE

```
  0.0 2
× 1 0
-------
  0.2 0   or   0.2
```

Multiply.

1. 0.002
× 10

2. 1.002
× 10

3. 0.3
× 100

4. 0.03
× 100

5. 0.003
× 100

6. 1.003
× 100

7. 0.4
× 200

8. 0.04
× 200

9. 0.004
× 200

10. 1.004
× 200

11. 0.5
× 300

12. 0.05
× 300

13. 0.005
× 300

14. 1.005
× 300

Rewrite each problem in vertical form, then multiply.

15. 0.06 × 10

16. 1.006 × 10

17. 0.07 × 500

18. 1.007 × 500

19. 0.08 × 600

20. 1.008 × 600

WORKED EXAMPLE

$$\begin{array}{r} \$4.87 \\ \times\ 16 \\ \hline 2922 \\ 487\ \ \\ \hline \$77.92 \end{array}$$

Multiply.

1. $\begin{array}{r} \$4.79 \\ \times\ 9 \\ \hline \end{array}$ **2.** $\begin{array}{r} \$2.63 \\ \times\ 7 \\ \hline \end{array}$

3. $\begin{array}{r} \$3.21 \\ \times\ 3 \\ \hline \end{array}$ **4.** $\begin{array}{r} \$6.27 \\ \times\ 25 \\ \hline \end{array}$ **5.** $\begin{array}{r} \$9.32 \\ \times\ 11 \\ \hline \end{array}$ **6.** $\begin{array}{r} \$4.03 \\ \times\ 30 \\ \hline \end{array}$

7. $\begin{array}{r} 29.3 \\ \times\ 89 \\ \hline \end{array}$ **8.** $\begin{array}{r} 0.456 \\ \times\ 73 \\ \hline \end{array}$ **9.** $\begin{array}{r} 8.79 \\ \times\ 64 \\ \hline \end{array}$ **10.** $\begin{array}{r} 0.808 \\ \times\ 97 \\ \hline \end{array}$

11. $\begin{array}{r} 81 \\ \times\ 1.3 \\ \hline \end{array}$ **12.** $\begin{array}{r} 17.32 \\ \times\ 5 \\ \hline \end{array}$ **13.** $\begin{array}{r} 35.4 \\ \times\ 101 \\ \hline \end{array}$ **14.** $\begin{array}{r} 91 \\ \times\ 2.2 \\ \hline \end{array}$

Rewrite each problem in vertical form, then multiply.

15. 65×1.7 **16.** 124×2.11

17. 6.23×6 **18.** 1372×0.17

19. 4726×0.006 **20.** 104×0.09

ANSWERS

1. $43.11
2. $18.41
3. $9.63
4. $156.75
5. $102.52
6. $120.90
7. 2607.7
8. 33.288
9. 562.56
10. 78.376
11. 105.3
12. 86.6
13. 3575.4
14. 200.2
15. 110.5
16. 261.64
17. 37.38
18. 233.24
19. 28.356
20. 9.36

ANSWERS

1. 0.968
2. 15.12
3. 41.676
4. 3389.17
5. 2.16
6. 0.495
7. 139.08
8. 5.31
9. 106.2
10. 0.096
11. 2918.4
12. 15.795
13. 1848.75
14. 51.85
15. 0.126
16. 0.046
17. 9.282
18. 58.77
19. 17.248
20. 3322.1

WORKED EXAMPLE

163×0.068

$$
\begin{array}{r}
163 \\
\times\, 0.068 \\
\hline
1304 \\
978 \\
\hline
11.084
\end{array}
$$

Multiply.

1.
$$\begin{array}{r} 986 \\ \times\, 0.001 \\ \hline \end{array}$$

2.
$$\begin{array}{r} 189 \\ \times\, 0.08 \\ \hline \end{array}$$

3.
$$\begin{array}{r} 1.812 \\ \times\, 23 \\ \hline \end{array}$$

4.
$$\begin{array}{r} 7211 \\ \times\, 0.47 \\ \hline \end{array}$$

5.
$$\begin{array}{r} 360 \\ \times\, 0.006 \\ \hline \end{array}$$

6.
$$\begin{array}{r} 495 \\ \times\, 0.001 \\ \hline \end{array}$$

7.
$$\begin{array}{r} 1.83 \\ \times\, 76 \\ \hline \end{array}$$

8.
$$\begin{array}{r} 0.118 \\ \times\, 45 \\ \hline \end{array}$$

9.
$$\begin{array}{r} 5.9 \\ \times\, 18 \\ \hline \end{array}$$

10.
$$\begin{array}{r} 0.048 \\ \times\, 2 \\ \hline \end{array}$$

11.
$$\begin{array}{r} 2432 \\ \times\, 1.2 \\ \hline \end{array}$$

12.
$$\begin{array}{r} 0.243 \\ \times\, 65 \\ \hline \end{array}$$

13.
$$\begin{array}{r} 255 \\ \times\, 7.25 \\ \hline \end{array}$$

14.
$$\begin{array}{r} 1037 \\ \times\, 0.05 \\ \hline \end{array}$$

Rewrite each problem in vertical form, then multiply.

15. 18×0.007

16. 23×0.002

17. 119×0.078

18. 653×0.09

19. 176×0.098

20. 478×6.95

436

OBJECTIVE   Skill 10   Multiply a decimal by a decimal.

SKILL MODEL

Multiply $4.2 \times 0.13 = ?$ **PROBLEM**	$\begin{array}{r} 4.2 \\ \times\, 0.13 \end{array}$	$\begin{array}{r} 4.2 \\ \times\, 0.13 \\ \hline 126 \\ 42 \\ \hline 546 \end{array}$	$\begin{array}{r} 4.2 \leftarrow \quad \text{1 place} \\ \times\, 0.13 \leftarrow +\,\text{2 places} \\ \hline 126 \\ 42 \\ \hline 0.546 \leftarrow \quad \text{3 places} \end{array}$	$\begin{array}{r} 4.2 \\ \times\, 0.13 \\ \hline 126 \\ 42 \\ \hline 0.546 \end{array}$ **ANSWER**

1   **2**   **3**   **4**

SOLUTION STEPS

Step 1   Write the multiplication problem in vertical form.

Step 2   Multiply as if the decimal numbers were whole numbers.

Step 3   Count the total number of decimal places in the problem. Write a decimal point in the answer so that the answer has the same total number of decimal places.

Step 4   Write the answer.

UNDERSTAND

$$\begin{array}{r} 4.2 \\ \times\, 0.13 \\ \hline 0.006 \end{array} \leftarrow \frac{3}{100} \times \frac{2}{10} = \frac{6}{1000}$$

$$0.12 \leftarrow \frac{3}{100} \times \frac{4}{1} = \frac{12}{100}$$

$$0.02 \leftarrow \frac{1}{10} \times \frac{2}{10} = \frac{2}{100}$$

$$\frac{+\,0.4}{0.546} \leftarrow \frac{1}{10} \times \frac{4}{1} = \frac{4}{10}$$

WORKED EXAMPLES

1. $\quad \begin{array}{r} 7.13 \\ \times\, 0.001 \\ \hline 0.00713 \end{array}$

2. $\begin{array}{r} 117.6 \\ \times\, 0.85 \\ \hline 5\,880 \\ 94\,08 \\ \hline 99.960 \end{array}$ or   99.96

3. $\quad 80.4 \times 4.03$

$$\begin{array}{r} 80.4 \\ \times\, 4.03 \\ \hline 2\,412 \\ 321\,60 \\ \hline 324.012 \end{array}$$

BRUSH-UP EXERCISES

1. $\begin{array}{r} 1.009 \\ \times\, 0.01 \\ \hline \end{array}$ **2.** $\begin{array}{r} 8.1 \\ \times\, 1.3 \\ \hline \end{array}$ **3.** $\begin{array}{r} 17.32 \\ \times\, 0.05 \\ \hline \end{array}$ **4.** $\begin{array}{r} 17.02 \\ \times\, 6.9 \\ \hline \end{array}$

5. 12.23×0.0066 **6.** 87.93×1.07

SELF-CHECK ANSWERS

1. 0.01009   **2.** 10.53   **3.** 0.866   **4.** 117.438   **5.** 0.080718   **6.** 94.0851

ANSWERS
1. 0.025
2. 0.052
3. 0.000059
4. 0.0063
5. 0.063
6. 0.363
7. 0.000059
8. 0.00059
9. 0.0059
10. 0.459
11. 0.69
12. 0.1001
13. 0.00081
14. 0.045
15. 0.0322
16. 0.8199
17. 0.30804
18. 2.64
19. 5.675
20. 0.000063

WORKED EXAMPLE

0.06×0.001

$$\begin{array}{r} 0.06 \\ \times\ 0.001 \\ \hline 0.00006 \end{array}$$

Multiply.

1. $\begin{array}{r} 0.01 \\ \times\ 2.5 \\ \hline \end{array}$ **2.** $\begin{array}{r} 0.52 \\ \times\ 0.1 \\ \hline \end{array}$

3. $\begin{array}{r} 0.059 \\ \times\ 0.001 \\ \hline \end{array}$ **4.** $\begin{array}{r} 0.63 \\ \times\ 0.01 \\ \hline \end{array}$ **5.** $\begin{array}{r} 0.63 \\ \times\ 0.1 \\ \hline \end{array}$ **6.** $\begin{array}{r} 3.63 \\ \times\ 0.1 \\ \hline \end{array}$

7. $\begin{array}{r} 0.059 \\ \times\ 0.001 \\ \hline \end{array}$ **8.** $\begin{array}{r} 0.059 \\ \times\ 0.01 \\ \hline \end{array}$ **9.** $\begin{array}{r} 0.059 \\ \times\ 0.1 \\ \hline \end{array}$ **10.** $\begin{array}{r} 4.59 \\ \times\ 0.1 \\ \hline \end{array}$

11. $\begin{array}{r} 1.38 \\ \times\ 0.5 \\ \hline \end{array}$ **12.** $\begin{array}{r} 2.002 \\ \times\ 0.05 \\ \hline \end{array}$ **13.** $\begin{array}{r} 0.006 \\ \times\ 0.135 \\ \hline \end{array}$ **14.** $\begin{array}{r} 0.03 \\ \times\ 1.5 \\ \hline \end{array}$

Rewrite each problem in vertical form, then multiply.

15. 16.1×0.002 **16.** 27.33×0.03

17. 18.12×0.017 **18.** 105.6×0.025

19. 113.5×0.05 **20.** 0.021×0.003

WORKED EXAMPLE
5.203 × 0.07
5.203
× 0.07
0.36421

Multiply.

1.   14.85
   × 0.7

2.   40.16
   × 0.06

3.   32.12
   × 4.4

4.   18.67
   × 0.21

5.   19.42
   × 0.37

6. 104.16
   × 4.41

7. 207.21
   × 3.21

8.   22.8
   × 1.3

9.   9.86
   × 1.5

10. 121.1
   × 2.5

11.   4.72
   × 0.7

12. 105.6
   × 0.75

13. 204.6
   × 0.5

14.   6.1
   × 1.7

Rewrite each problem in vertical form, then multiply.

15. 1.83 × 10.2

16. 0.08 × 2.7

17. 5.8 × 3.52

18. 2.6 × 1.83

19. 0.85 × 5.8

20. 83.7 × 7.5

ANSWERS
1. 10.395
2. 2.4096
3. 141.328
4. 3.9207
5. 7.1854
6. 459.3456
7. 665.1441
8. 29.64
9. 14.79
10. 302.75
11. 3.304
12. 79.2
13. 102.3
14. 10.37
15. 18.666
16. 0.216
17. 20.416
18. 4.758
19. 4.93
20. 627.75

ANSWERS
1. 0.2002
2. 0.04675
3. 0.1812
4. 0.7803
5. 24.915
6. 56.5614
7. 1.656
8. 5.05512
9. 3.6197
10. 0.447469
11. 168.053
12. 108.048
13. 163.2204
14. 292.572
15. 1.14595
16. 0.26164
17. 0.38675
18. 0.054009
19. 233.05572
20. 313.46345

WORKED EXAMPLE

$$\begin{array}{r} 0.0037 \\ \times\ 0.2 \\ \hline 0.00074 \end{array}$$

Multiply.

1.
$$\begin{array}{r} 0.091 \\ \times\ 2.2 \end{array}$$

2.
$$\begin{array}{r} 0.0374 \\ \times\ 1.25 \end{array}$$

3.
$$\begin{array}{r} 3.02 \\ \times\ 0.06 \end{array}$$

4.
$$\begin{array}{r} 26.01 \\ \times\ 0.03 \end{array}$$

5.
$$\begin{array}{r} 8.25 \\ \times\ 3.02 \end{array}$$

6.
$$\begin{array}{r} 14.07 \\ \times\ 4.02 \end{array}$$

7.
$$\begin{array}{r} 0.72 \\ \times\ 2.3 \end{array}$$

8.
$$\begin{array}{r} 0.504 \\ \times\ 10.03 \end{array}$$

9.
$$\begin{array}{r} 1.0342 \\ \times\ 3.50 \end{array}$$

10.
$$\begin{array}{r} 0.209 \\ \times\ 2.141 \end{array}$$

11.
$$\begin{array}{r} 21.004 \\ \times\ 8.001 \end{array}$$

12.
$$\begin{array}{r} 18.002 \\ \times\ 6.002 \end{array}$$

13.
$$\begin{array}{r} 16.002 \\ \times\ 10.200 \end{array}$$

14.
$$\begin{array}{r} 24.30 \\ \times\ 12.04 \end{array}$$

Rewrite each problem in vertical form, then multiply.

15. 0.65 × 1.763

16. 0.124 × 2.11

17. 11.05 × 0.035

18. 36.006 × 0.0015

19. 19.21 × 12.132

20. 24.034 × 13.0425

OBJECTIVE   Skill 11   Divide a decimal by a whole number.

SKILL MODEL

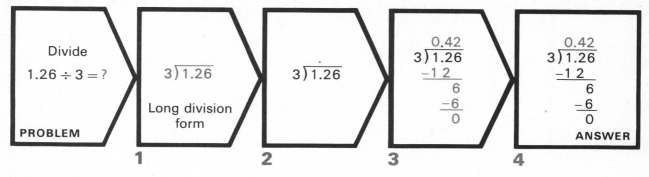

PROBLEM

Divide
$1.26 \div 3 = ?$

1

$3\overline{)1.26}$

Long division
form

2

$3\overline{)1.26}$

3

$$\begin{array}{r} 0.42 \\ 3\overline{)1.26} \\ \underline{-1\,2} \\ 6 \\ \underline{-6} \\ 0 \end{array}$$

4

$$\begin{array}{r} 0.42 \\ 3\overline{)1.26} \\ \underline{-1\,2} \\ 6 \\ \underline{-6} \\ 0 \end{array}$$

ANSWER

SOLUTION STEPS

Step 1   Write the division problem in long division form.

Step 2   Write the decimal point for the answer directly above the decimal point in the problem.

Step 3   Divide.

Step 4   Write the answer; add a zero in the ones places if necessary.

UNDERSTAND

$$\begin{array}{r} 0.42 \\ 3\overline{)1.26} \\ \underline{-1.2} \quad \leftarrow \quad 3 \times \frac{4}{10} = \frac{12}{10} \\ 6 \\ \underline{-6} \quad \leftarrow \quad 3 \times \frac{2}{100} = \frac{6}{100} \\ 0 \end{array}$$

WORKED EXAMPLES

1.
$$\begin{array}{r} 0.075 \\ 12\overline{)0.900} \\ \underline{-84} \\ 60 \\ \underline{-60} \\ 0 \end{array}$$

2.
$$\begin{array}{r} 0.532 \\ 20\overline{)10.640} \\ \underline{-10\,0} \\ 64 \\ \underline{-60} \\ 40 \\ \underline{-40} \\ 0 \end{array}$$

3. $20.4 \div 17$

$$\begin{array}{r} 1.2 \\ 17\overline{)20.4} \\ \underline{-17} \\ 3\,4 \\ \underline{-3\,4} \\ 0 \end{array}$$

BRUSH-UP EXERCISES

1. $12\overline{)11.88}$

2. $59\overline{)212.4}$

3. $10\overline{)63.50}$

4. $0.324 \div 24$

SELF-CHECK ANSWERS

1. 0.99   **2.** 3.6   **3.** 6.35   **4.** 0.0135

ANSWERS
1. 0.2
2. 0.02
3. 0.03
4. 2.33
5. 2.011
6. 20.107
7. 0.02
8. 0.378
9. 0.002
10. 0.023
11. 1.9
12. 3.5
13. 2.25
14. 2.4
15. 0.227
16. 8.034
17. 3.5
18. 0.24
19. 0.024
20. 0.022

WORKED EXAMPLE

$$\begin{array}{r} 8.4 \\ 6\overline{)50.4} \\ -48 \\ \hline 2\,4 \\ -2\,4 \\ \hline 0 \end{array}$$

Divide.

1. $4\overline{)0.8}$ **2.** $4\overline{)0.08}$

3. $8\overline{)0.24}$ **4.** $3\overline{)6.99}$ **5.** $6\overline{)12.066}$ **6.** $6\overline{)120.642}$

7. $12\overline{)0.24}$ **8.** $25\overline{)9.450}$ **9.** $12\overline{)0.024}$ **10.** $42\overline{)0.966}$

11. $25\overline{)47.5}$ **12.** $21\overline{)73.5}$ **13.** $30\overline{)67.50}$ **14.** $34\overline{)81.6}$

Rewrite each problem in vertical form, then divide.

15. $0.454 \div 2$ **16.** $48.204 \div 6$

17. $73.5 \div 21$ **18.** $8.16 \div 34$

19. $0.816 \div 34$ **20.** $0.660 \div 30$

<table>
<tr><td>

WORKED EXAMPLE

$$
\begin{array}{r}
0.32 \\
10\overline{)3.20} \\
-30 \\
\hline
20 \\
-20 \\
\hline
0
\end{array}
$$

</td></tr>
</table>

Divide.

1. $10\overline{)80.6}$ **2.** $100\overline{)0.67}$

3. $10\overline{)18.7}$ **4.** $400\overline{)9.6}$ **5.** $20\overline{)86.4}$ **6.** $200\overline{)6.4}$

7. $40\overline{)16.16}$ **8.** $10\overline{)100.6}$ **9.** $50\overline{)0.8}$ **10.** $500\overline{)0.5}$

11. $1000\overline{)806.3}$ **12.** $200\overline{)10.8}$ **13.** $60\overline{)0.6}$ **14.** $10\overline{)8.7}$

Rewrite each problem in vertical form, then divide.

15. $8.632 \div 20$ **16.** $0.203 \div 10$

17. $1.9 \div 100$ **18.** $9.75 \div 2000$

19. $117.6 \div 4$ **20.** $8.97 \div 1000$

ANSWERS

1. 8.06

2. 0.0067

3. 1.87

4. 0.024

5. 4.32

6. 0.032

7. 0.404

8. 10.06

9. 0.016

10. 0.001

11. 0.8063

12. 0.054

13. 0.01

14. 0.87

15. 0.4316

16. 0.0203

17. 0.019

18. 0.004875

19. 29.4

20. 0.00897

ANSWERS

1. 1.005
2. 0.305
3. 40.15
4. 200.06
5. 23.05
6. 40.5
7. 0.608
8. 5.02
9. 0.065
10. 5.08
11. 11.78
12. 7.05
13. 0.104
14. 103.4
15. 7.05
16. 0.806
17. 97.524
18. 11.05
19. 7.08
20. 0.132

WORKED EXAMPLE

$$17)\overline{5.168}$$ gives 0.304
$$-5\ 1$$
$$6$$
$$-0$$
$$68$$
$$-68$$
$$0$$

Divide.

1. $22)\overline{22.11}$ 2. $18)\overline{5.49}$

3. $44)\overline{1766.6}$ 4. $15)\overline{3000.9}$ 5. $8)\overline{184.4}$ 6. $86)\overline{3483}$

7. $50)\overline{30.4}$ 8. $15)\overline{75.3}$ 9. $56)\overline{3.64}$ 10. $45)\overline{228.6}$

11. $25)\overline{294.5}$ 12. $88)\overline{620.4}$ 13. $85)\overline{8.84}$ 14. $75)\overline{7755}$

Rewrite vertically and then divide.

15. $253.8 \div 36$ 16. $44.33 \div 55$

17. $2438.1 \div 25$ 18. $176.8 \div 16$

19. $672.6 \div 95$ 20. $8.58 \div 65$

OBJECTIVE   Skill 12   Divide a decimal by a decimal.

SKILL MODEL

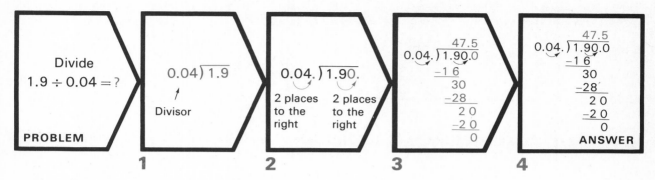

PROBLEM   **1**   **2**   **3**   **4**   ANSWER

SOLUTION STEPS

Step 1   Write the division problem in long division form.

Step 2   Count the number of decimal places in the divisor. Move both decimal points in the problem that number of places to the right. Add zeros if necessary.

Step 3   Write the decimal point in the answer space directly above the new decimal point. Divide; carry to three decimal places, if necessary.

Step 4   Write the answer.

WHY IT WORKS

$$0.04\overline{)1.9} = \frac{1.9}{0.04} = \frac{1.9}{0.04} \times \frac{100}{100} = \frac{190}{4}$$

$$\frac{190}{4} = 4\overline{)190}$$

Notice that the divisor becomes a whole number.

WORKED EXAMPLES

1.
$$
\begin{array}{r}
3.0 \quad \text{or} \quad 3 \\
2.1\,\overline{)6.3.0} \\
-6\,3\,0 \\
\hline
0
\end{array}
$$

2.
$$
\begin{array}{r}
10.4 \\
0.0850.\,\overline{)0.8840.0} \\
-850 \\
\hline
340\,0 \\
-340\,0 \\
\hline
0
\end{array}
$$

3. $10.64 \div 3.5$
$$
\begin{array}{r}
3.04 \\
3.5.\,\overline{)10.6.40} \\
-10\,5 \\
\hline
1\,40 \\
-1\,40 \\
\hline
0
\end{array}
$$

BRUSH-UP EXERCISES

1. $3.5\overline{)70.35}$ 2. $28.6\overline{)1481.48}$ 3. $2.78\overline{)31.553}$ 4. $3.552 \div 0.0024$

SELF-CHECK ANSWERS

1. 20.1   2. 51.8   3. 11.35   4. 1480

ANSWERS
1. 200
2. 800
3. 1011
4. 431
5. 703
6. 801
7. 3007
8. 31,042
9. 12,071
10. 8201
11. 78
12. 355
13. 107
14. 1032
15. 902
16. 207
17. 21,042
18. 5109
19. 284
20. 2530

WORKED EXAMPLE

$$0.09.\overline{)10.98.} = \frac{122.}{} = 122$$

```
         122. = 122
0.09.) 10.98.
        -9
        19
       -18
        18
       -18
         0
```

Divide.

1. $0.08\overline{)16}$ **2.** $0.05\overline{)40}$

3. $0.05\overline{)50.55}$ **4.** $0.03\overline{)12.93}$ **5.** $0.07\overline{)49.21}$ **6.** $0.08\overline{)64.08}$

7. $0.005\overline{)15.035}$ **8.** $0.003\overline{)93.126}$ **9.** $0.006\overline{)72.426}$ **10.** $0.004\overline{)32.804}$

11. $0.027\overline{)2.106}$ **12.** $0.023\overline{)8.165}$ **13.** $0.038\overline{)4.066}$ **14.** $0.021\overline{)21.672}$

Rewrite each problem in vertical form, then divide.

15. $81.18 \div 0.09$ **16.** $14.49 \div 0.07$

17. $84.168 \div 0.004$ **18.** $30.654 \div 0.006$

19. $74.692 \div 0.263$ **20.** $852.61 \div 0.337$

WORKED EXAMPLE

$$
\begin{array}{r}
2.4 \\
0.6\overline{)1.4.4} \\
-1\,2 \\
\hline
2\,4 \\
-2\,4 \\
\hline
0
\end{array}
$$

Divide.

1. $0.7\overline{)4.62}$ **2.** $0.3\overline{)1.71}$

3. $1.3\overline{)6.89}$ **4.** $2.7\overline{)4.86}$ **5.** $4.6\overline{)8.28}$ **6.** $2.5\overline{)4.25}$

7. $5.3\overline{)24.38}$ **8.** $6.1\overline{)42.09}$ **9.** $4.5\overline{)42.30}$ **10.** $6.3\overline{)14.49}$

11. $10.4\overline{)100.88}$ **12.** $12.7\overline{)109.22}$ **13.** $15.6\overline{)117.00}$ **14.** $21.3\overline{)157.62}$

Rewrite each problem in vertical form, then divide.

15. $17.92 \div 5.6$ **16.** $28.22 \div 8.3$

17. $365.81 \div 15.7$ **18.** $146.88 \div 14.4$

19. $171.36 \div 25.2$ **20.** $374.88 \div 42.6$

ANSWERS
1. 6.6
2. 5.7
3. 5.3
4. 1.8
5. 1.8
6. 1.7
7. 4.6
8. 6.9
9. 9.4
10. 2.3
11. 9.7
12. 8.6
13. 7.5
14. 7.4
15. 3.2
16. 3.4
17. 23.3
18. 10.2
19. 6.8
20. 8.8

ANSWERS	
1.	5.1
2.	9.6
3.	2.8
4.	3.4
5.	2.6
6.	3.7
7.	6.2
8.	3.9
9.	0.25
10.	0.43
11.	0.02
12.	0.2
13.	0.07
14.	0.03
15.	8.13
16.	4.71
17.	13.8
18.	21.3
19.	1.04
20.	3.38
21.	0.09
22.	6.71

Divide.

1. $0.26\overline{)1.326}$ **2.** $0.17\overline{)1.632}$ **3.** $0.64\overline{)1.792}$ **4.** $0.91\overline{)3.094}$

5. $3.21\overline{)8.346}$ **6.** $2.41\overline{)8.917}$ **7.** $1.44\overline{)8.928}$ **8.** $2.46\overline{)9.594}$

9. $0.17\overline{)0.0425}$ **10.** $0.23\overline{)0.0989}$ **11.** $0.31\overline{)0.0062}$ **12.** $0.42\overline{)0.084}$

13. $4.62\overline{)0.3234}$ **14.** $7.34\overline{)0.2202}$ **15.** $2.78\overline{)22.6014}$ **16.** $5.26\overline{)24.7746}$

Rewrite each problem in vertical form, then divide.

17. $2.484 \div 0.18$ **18.** $4.473 \div 0.21$

19. $1.2168 \div 1.17$ **20.** $8.3148 \div 2.46$

21. $0.7767 \div 8.63$ **22.** $28.9872 \div 4.32$

Divide.

1. $6.4\overline{)6.72}$ 2. $1.5\overline{)31.2}$ 3. $0.06\overline{)0.183}$ 4. $0.07\overline{)0.1204}$

5. $0.5\overline{)0.0102}$ 6. $4.05\overline{)32.643}$ 7. $0.008\overline{)0.1284}$ 8. $8.5\overline{)26.367}$

9. $11.5\overline{)58.42}$ 10. $4.4\overline{)26.818}$ 11. $5.5\overline{)60.61}$ 12. $10.5\overline{)21.84}$

13. $9.6\overline{)87.024}$ 14. $0.15\overline{)2.712}$ 15. $0.075\overline{)0.3795}$ 16. $1.2\overline{)252.6}$

Rewrite each problem in vertical form, then divide.

17. $5.603 \div 0.05$ 18. $3719.61 \div 18.5$

19. $0.00603 \div 0.06$ 20. $160.8402 \div 8.04$

21. $15.678 \div 1.95$ 22. $11.6424 \div 1.05$

ANSWERS

1. 1.05
2. 20.8
3. 3.05
4. 1.72
5. 0.0204
6. 8.06
7. 16.05
8. 3.102
9. 5.08
10. 6.095
11. 11.02
12. 2.08
13. 9.065
14. 18.08
15. 5.06
16. 210.5
17. 112.06
18. 201.06
19. 0.1005
20. 20.005
21. 8.04
22. 11.088

449

SKILL 9

1. 105.56
2. 10176.3
3. 6600.88
4. 9721.873
5. 4549.77
6. 722.133

SKILL 9

1. 15.08 × 7
2. 376.9 × 27
3. 150.02 × 44
4. 47.891 × 203
5. 56.17 × 81
6. 5.871 × 123

SKILL 10

1. 41.174
2. 68.3753
3. 2078.08
4. 2.107689
5. 1.166208
6. 2193.6375

SKILL 10

1. 58.82 × 0.7
2. 12.901 × 5.3
3. 152.8 × 13.6
4. 5.871 × 0.359
5. 6.074 × 0.192
6. 138.75 × 15.81

SKILL 11

1. 6.31
2. 2.72
3. 5.678
4. 5.7
5. 4.44
6. 2.008

SKILL 11

1. 5)31.55
2. 18)48.96
3. 21)119.238
4. 132)752.4
5. 159.84 ÷ 36
6. 283.128 ÷ 141

SKILL 12

1. 1.45
2. 4.1
3. 0.416
4. 2.11
5. 8.7
6. 9.45

SKILL 12

1. 0.28)0.406
2. 3.21)13.161
3. 12.5)5.2
4. 67.61)142.6571
5. 0.3306 ÷ 0.038
6. 16.065 ÷ 1.7

DECIMALS
Unit Mastery Test – Page 1
Answers on Page 541

SKILL 1   Write as decimals.

1. 8 and 73 hundredths

2. 75 and 276 ten-thousandths

3. nine hundred two and six thousandths

SKILL 2

1. Round 8.526 to the nearest hundredth.

2. Round 5.0489 to the nearest tenth.

3. Round 9.8396 to the nearest thousandth.

SKILL 3   Write as decimals.

1. $7\frac{15}{100}$

2. $\frac{5}{16}$

3. $1\frac{5}{8}$

SKILL 4   Write as a fraction or mixed number in lowest terms.

1. 0.7

2. 16.14

3. 21.325

SKILL 5

1. $ 12.20
    + 210.16

2.   124.331
       10.2
    +   3.12

3. 8.62 + 61.103

SKILL 6

1. $ 64.21
    + 370.99

2.   218.706
       8.69
    + 24.048

3. 26.764 + 4.87

SKILL 1

1.

2.

3.

SKILL 2

1.

2.

3.

SKILL 3

1.

2.

3.

SKILL 4

1.

2.

3.

SKILL 5

1.

2.

3.

SKILL 6

1.

2.

3.

SKILL 7

1.

2.

3.

SKILL 8

1.

2.

3.

SKILL 9

1.

2.

3.

SKILL 10

1.

2.

3.

SKILL 11

1.

2.

3.

SKILL 12

1.

2.

3.

SKILL 7

1. $267.89
     −   43.21

2.   674.487
     − 120.04

3. 67.48 − 4.2

SKILL 8

1. $727.48
     − 249.69

2.   206.1437
     − 29.1529

3. 82.1 − 6.738

SKILL 9

1. 10.09
     × 9

2. 381.5
     × 53

3. 32.875 × 504

SKILL 10

1. 31.22
     × 0.3

2. 12.01
     × 7.02

3. 450.50 × 678

SKILL 11

1. 21$)\overline{4.2}$

2. 60$)\overline{30.3}$

3. 42.21 ÷ 14

SKILL 12

1. 0.15$)\overline{1.245}$

2. 27.6$)\overline{41.4}$

3. 575.7 ÷ 9.5

UNIT 11
PROPORTIONS

Skill 1   Write ratios in simplest form, using "TO",
a colon (:), or a fraction.

Skill 2   Write rates in simplest form, using a fraction.

Skill 3   Find unit rates.

Skill 4   Determine if proportions are true.

Skill 5   Solve true proportions.

Skill 6   Write equal rates as a proportion, then solve.

SKILL 1 Write each ratio as a fraction in simplest form.

1. 70 lb to 20 lb **2.** 48 g to 18 g **3.** 1 hr 15 min to 45 min

SKILL 2 Write each rate in simplest form, using a fraction.

1. 150 km on 20 L **2.** $75 for 30 hr **3.** 154 mi in 6 hr

SKILL 3 Find the unit rate for each problem. Round to the nearest tenth or cent.

1. $18.00 for 4 lb **2.** 24 sales in 5 days **3.** 560 km in 15 hr

SKILL 1

1.

2.

3.

SKILL 2

1.

2.

3.

SKILL 3

1.

2.

3.

Unit Diagnostic Test – Page 2

Answers on Page 541

SKILL 4   Tell if each proportion is TRUE (T) or NOT TRUE (NT).

SKILL 4

1. $\dfrac{6}{8} \overset{?}{=} \dfrac{54}{72}$

2. $\dfrac{11}{12} \overset{?}{=} \dfrac{16}{18}$

3. $\dfrac{32}{48} \overset{?}{=} \dfrac{512}{768}$

1.

2.

3.

SKILL 5   Find the unknown value in each proportion. Check the answer.

SKILL 5

1. $\dfrac{7}{8} = \dfrac{s}{96}$

2. $\dfrac{n}{24} = \dfrac{299}{312}$

3. $\dfrac{1}{d} = \dfrac{16}{3120}$

1.

2.

3.

$s = \underline{\qquad}$

$n = \underline{\qquad}$

$d = \underline{\qquad}$

SKILL 6   Write each proportion. Solve for the unknown and write the corresponding rate.

SKILL 6

1. 64 km on 2 L = s km on 8 L

2. 320 ft in 6 hr = x ft in 18 hr

3. t dollars saved in 12 months = \$720 saved in 5 months

1.

2.

3.

$s = \underline{\qquad}$

$x = \underline{\qquad}$

$t = \underline{\qquad}$

rate: _____

rate: _____

rate: _____

OBJECTIVE Skill 1 Write ratios in simplest form, using "TO", a colon (:), or a fraction.

SKILL MODEL

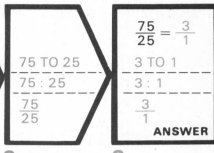

1 hr 15 min to 25 min Write this relationship as a ratio in simplest form, using "TO", a colon (:), and a fraction. **PROBLEM**	Since 1 hr and 15 min = 60 min + 15 min = 75 min the relationship becomes 75 min to 25 min

1

75 TO 25
75 : 25
$\frac{75}{25}$

2

$\frac{75}{25} = \frac{3}{1}$
3 TO 1
3 : 1
$\frac{3}{1}$
ANSWER

3

SOLUTION STEPS

Step 1 Rewrite the relationship so that both quantities have the same units. Use the conversion chart on the inside back cover as needed.

Step 2 Write the ratio using "TO", a colon, and a fraction. The ratio itself is expressed without units.

Step 3 Reduce the fraction in Step 2 to lowest terms. Use the numbers in this fraction to write the three answers in simplest form.

> **REMEMBER**
>
> A ratio is a comparison of two quantities having the <u>same units</u>. The ratios 3 TO 1, 3 : 1, and $\frac{3}{1}$ are all read as "three to one".
>
> A ratio is in <u>simplest form</u> when the fraction is in lowest terms.

WORKED EXAMPLES

MONTHLY BUDGET		
Salary	Rent	Food
$700	$280	$200

1. Food-to-salary ratio

$\frac{200 \text{ dollars}}{700 \text{ dollars}} = \frac{2}{7}$

2 TO 7
2 : 7

2. Rent-to-salary ratio

$\frac{280 \text{ dollars}}{700 \text{ dollars}} = \frac{2}{5}$

2 TO 5
2 : 5

3. 8 km to 150 m
(8 km = 8000 m)

$\frac{8000 \text{ m}}{150 \text{ m}} = \frac{160}{3}$

160 TO 3
160 : 3

BRUSH-UP EXERCISES

Compare the numbers in the table by writing a ratio in simplest form. Use the conversion chart on the inside back cover as needed.

DIMENSIONS OF A ROOM		
Length	Width	Height
20 ft	14 ft	11 ft 3 in

1. Length-to-width ratio **2.** Length-to-height ratio **3.** Height-to-width ratio

SELF-CHECK ANSWERS

1. $\frac{10}{7}$ or 10 TO 7 or 10 : 7 **2.** $\frac{16}{9}$ or 16 TO 9 or 16 : 9 **3.** $\frac{45}{56}$ or 45 TO 56 or 45 : 56

Compare the numbers in the table by writing a ratio as a fraction in lowest terms.

Stereo Store Owner's Working Schedule			
Sales	Repairs	Delivery	Bookkeeping
4 hr	2 hr	3 hr	2 hr

1. Bookkeeping-Sales ratio:

2. Repairs-Delivery ratio:

3. Sales-Repair ratio:

4. Delivery-Repairs ratio:

5. Sales-Delivery ratio:

6. Delivery-Bookkeeping ratio:

km Driven				
Mon.	Tues.	Wed.	Thurs.	Fri.
700	820	883	850	1070

7. Mon.-Tues. ratio:

8. Mon.-Wed. ratio:

9. Mon.-Thurs. ratio:

10. Mon.-Fri. ratio:

11. Tues.-Wed. ratio:

12. Tues.-Thurs. ratio:

13. Tues.-Fri. ratio:

14. Wed.-Thurs. ratio:

15. Wed.-Fri. ratio:

16. Thurs.-Fri. ratio:

Carpenter's Weekly Work Expenses			
Food	Transportation	Supplies	Tools
$16.40	$12.40	$3.60	$8.75

17. Food-Transportation ratio:

18. Food-Supplies ratio:

19. Food-Tools ratio:

20. Transportation-Supplies ratio:

21. Transportation-Tools ratio:

22. Supplies-Tools ratio:

ANSWERS

1. $\frac{1}{2}$
2. $\frac{2}{3}$
3. $\frac{2}{1}$
4. $\frac{3}{2}$
5. $\frac{4}{3}$
6. $\frac{3}{2}$
7. $\frac{35}{41}$
8. $\frac{700}{883}$
9. $\frac{14}{17}$
10. $\frac{70}{107}$
11. $\frac{820}{883}$
12. $\frac{82}{85}$
13. $\frac{82}{107}$
14. $\frac{883}{850}$
15. $\frac{883}{1070}$
16. $\frac{85}{107}$
17. $\frac{41}{31}$
18. $\frac{41}{9}$
19. $\frac{328}{175}$
20. $\frac{31}{9}$
21. $\frac{248}{175}$
22. $\frac{72}{175}$

Complete the following table.
See inside back cover for
necessary conversions.

	Ratio	Express the ratio in simplest form TO	:	Fraction
1.	675 m to 50 m	27 TO 2		
2.	36 km to 8 km	9 TO 2		
3.	5 lb to 1 lb 14 oz	8 TO 3		
4.	255 L to 21 L		85 : 7	
5.	16 g to 5 g		16 : 5	
6.	8 yd to 12 ft		2 : 1	
7.	$16.00 to $10.00	8 TO 5		
8.	255 m to 45 m	17 TO 3		
9.	350 mL to 1 L	7 TO 20		
10.	2 oz to 2 lb	1 TO 16		
11.	520 g to 2 kg	13 TO 50		
12.	$5.00 to $3.50	10 TO 7		
13.	68 m to 36 m		17 : 9	
14.	3 yd to 2 ft 8 in		27 : 8	

Complete the table. Write each ratio in simplest form. See inside back cover for necessary conversions.

ANSWERS
1. 17 TO 3; 17 : 3; $\frac{17}{3}$
2. 50 TO 3; 50 : 3; $\frac{50}{3}$
3. 30 TO 7; 30 : 7; $\frac{30}{7}$
4. 6 TO 1; 6 : 1; $\frac{6}{1}$
5. 13 TO 9; 13 : 9; $\frac{13}{9}$
6. 43 TO 50; 43 : 50; $\frac{43}{50}$
7. 43 TO 50; 43 : 50; $\frac{43}{50}$
8. 1 TO 73; 1 : 73; $\frac{1}{73}$
9. 4 TO 13; 4 : 13; $\frac{4}{13}$
10. 18 TO 5; 18 : 5; $\frac{18}{5}$
11. 14 TO 125; 14 : 125; $\frac{14}{125}$
12. 16 TO 7; 16 : 7; $\frac{16}{7}$
13. 225 TO 1; 225 : 1; $\frac{225}{1}$
14. 231 TO 2; 231 : 2; $\frac{231}{2}$

WORKED EXAMPLE

18¢ to $2.07

18¢ to 207¢

$$\frac{18}{207} = \frac{2}{23}$$

2 TO 23 or 2 : 23 or $\frac{2}{23}$

	Ratio	Express the ratio in simplest form		
		TO	:	Fraction
1.	136 in to 24 in			
2.	1 L to 60 mL			
3.	15 min to 3 min 30 sec			
4.	15 qt to 5 pt			
5.	$45.50 to $31.50			
6.	860 mm to 1 m			
7.	860 m to 1 km			
8.	3¢ to $2.19			
9.	16 miles to 52 miles			
10.	$1\frac{1}{2}$ days to 10 hr			
11.	56 g to $\frac{1}{2}$ kg			
12.	0.08 L to 35 mL			
13.	1 hr to 16 sec			
14.	$3\frac{1}{2}$ mi to 160 ft			

LESSON PROPORTIONS Skill 2

OBJECTIVE Skill 2 Write rates in simplest form, using a fraction.

SKILL MODEL

765 miles on 27 gallons of gas

Write this as a rate in simplest form.

PROBLEM

$\frac{765 \text{ mi}}{27 \text{ gal}}$

1

$\frac{765}{27} \frac{\text{mi}}{\text{gal}}$

$\frac{765 \div 9}{27 \div 9} = \frac{85}{3}$

2

$\frac{85 \text{ mi}}{3 \text{ gal}}$

ANSWER

3

SOLUTION STEPS

Step 1 Write the two quantities in a fraction. Make sure to include the units.

Step 2 Consider the number part of the fraction. Reduce this to lowest terms.

Step 3 Write the reduced fraction together with the original units. This is your answer in simplest form.

REMEMBER

A rate is a comparison of two quantities having <u>different</u> <u>units</u>. A rate is not complete without the units.

— — — — — — — — — — — — — — —

A rate is in <u>simplest</u> <u>form</u> when the fraction is in lowest terms.

WORKED EXAMPLES

1. 10 eggs make 4 omelettes

$= \frac{10 \text{ eggs}}{4 \text{ omelettes}}$

$= \frac{5 \text{ eggs}}{2 \text{ omelettes}}$

2. $50 for 8 hr work

$= \frac{50 \text{ dollars}}{8 \text{ hr}}$

$= \frac{25 \text{ dollars}}{4 \text{ hr}}$

3. 2002 km in 39 hr

$= \frac{2002 \text{ km}}{39 \text{ hr}}$

$= \frac{154 \text{ km}}{3 \text{ hr}}$

BRUSH-UP EXERCISES

Write as rates in simplest form, using a fraction.

1. 100 calories in 6 oz

2. 170 km on 8 L of gas

3. 1239 students in 15 classes

SELF-CHECK ANSWERS

1. $\frac{50 \text{ cal}}{3 \text{ oz}}$ **2.** $\frac{85 \text{ km}}{4 \text{ L}}$ **3.** $\frac{413 \text{ students}}{5 \text{ classes}}$

461

ANSWERS

1. $\dfrac{239 \text{ km}}{1 \text{ day}}$

2. $\dfrac{37 \text{ km}}{1 \text{ L}}$

3. $\dfrac{10 \text{ m}}{1 \text{ sec}}$

4. $\dfrac{100 \text{ m}}{11 \text{ sec}}$

5. $\dfrac{23 \text{ cal}}{2 \text{ min}}$

6. $\dfrac{5 \text{ gal}}{\$2}$

7. $\dfrac{7 \text{ g}}{2 \text{ min}}$

8. $\dfrac{\$27}{4 \text{ L}}$

9. $\dfrac{3 \text{ g}}{\$2}$

10. $\dfrac{111 \text{ mi}}{2 \text{ hr}}$

11. $\dfrac{307 \text{ m}}{20 \text{ sec}}$

12. $\dfrac{\$189}{5 \text{ g}}$

13. $\dfrac{31 \text{ mi}}{2 \text{ gal}}$

14. $\dfrac{1482 \text{ mi}}{7 \text{ days}}$

WORKED EXAMPLE

645 km in 9 hr

$$\dfrac{645 \text{ km}}{9 \text{ hr}}$$

$$\dfrac{215 \text{ km}}{3 \text{ hr}}$$

Write each rate as a fraction in lowest terms. Be sure to include the proper units.

1. 239 km in 1 day

2. 37 km on 1 L

3. 100 m in 10 sec

4. 200 m in 22 sec

5. 115 calories in 10 min

6. 15 gallons for $6

7. 42 g in 12 min

8. $54 for 8 L

9. 18 g for $12

10. 333 mi in 6 hr

11. 921 m in 60 sec

12. $756 for 20 g

13. 310 mi on 20 gallons

14. 7410 mi in 35 days

WORKED EXAMPLE

105 transistors in 10 days

$$\frac{105 \text{ transistors}}{10 \text{ days}}$$

$$\frac{21 \text{ transistors}}{2 \text{ days}}$$

Write each rate as a fraction in lowest terms. Be sure to include the proper units.

1. 720 filters in 1 day

2. 64 sales in 6 days

3. 56 people in 10 rows

4. 70 photos on 8 pages

5. 7 hits in 2 games

6. 8 doctors for 140 patients

7. 58 houses in 8 blocks

8. 4 tickets for $18

9. 48 commercials in 5 hr

10. 90 points in 4 games

11. 8 weeks for $260

12. 50 rooms on 4 floors

13. 15 repairs for $370

14. 325 people in 15 buses

Write each rate as a fraction in lowest terms. Be sure to include the proper units.

ANSWERS

1. $\dfrac{27 \text{ km}}{1 \text{ hr}}$
2. $\dfrac{50 \text{ m}}{27 \text{ sec}}$
3. $\dfrac{5 \text{ gal}}{\$6}$
4. $\dfrac{3 \text{ kg}}{7 \text{ min}}$
5. $\dfrac{17 \text{ km}}{2 \text{ L}}$
6. $\dfrac{69 \text{ g}}{2 \text{ hr}}$
7. $\dfrac{2 \text{ mi}}{5 \text{ min}}$
8. $\dfrac{7 \text{ ft}}{\$13}$
9. $\dfrac{15 \text{ flights}}{2 \text{ days}}$
10. $\dfrac{5 \text{ cars}}{3 \text{ garages}}$
11. $\dfrac{15 \text{ g protein}}{2 \text{ hot dogs}}$
12. $\dfrac{\$65}{6 \text{ records}}$
13. $\dfrac{5 \text{ passengers}}{2 \text{ taxis}}$
14. $\dfrac{28 \text{ TV sets}}{15 \text{ houses}}$
15. $\dfrac{65 \text{ problems}}{4 \text{ pages}}$
16. $\dfrac{36 \text{ people}}{7 \text{ families}}$

1. 54 km in 2 hr
2. 100 m in 54 sec
3. 10 gal for $12
4. 15 kg in 35 min
5. 34 km on 4 L
6. 207 g in 6 hr
7. 16 mi in 40 min
8. 42 ft for $78
9. 60 flights in 8 days
10. 20 cars in 12 garages
11. 30 g protein in 4 hot dogs
12. $65 for 6 records
13. 110 passengers in 44 taxis
14. 56 TV sets in 30 houses
15. 260 problems on 16 pages
16. 72 people in 14 families

OBJECTIVE   Skill 3   Find unit rates.

SKILL MODEL

$12.42 for 6 pounds of ground beef

Find the unit rate.

PROBLEM

1

$$\frac{12.42 \text{ dollars}}{6 \text{ pounds}}$$

2

$$\frac{12.42}{6} \quad \frac{\text{dollars}}{\text{pounds}}$$

$$\frac{12.42 \div 6}{6 \div 6} = \frac{2.07}{1}$$

3

$$\frac{2.07 \text{ dollars}}{1 \text{ pound}}$$

OR

$2.07 per pound

ANSWER

SOLUTION STEPS

Step 1   Write the given rate as a fraction. Make sure to insert the units.

Step 2   Consider the number part of the fraction only. Divide the numerator and denominator by the number in the denominator, so that the new fraction will have 1 in its denominator.

Step 3   Write the fraction in Step 2 together with the original units. Then express the quantity using the word "per". This is the answer.

> **REMEMBER**
>
> The most useful type of rate is a <u>unit rate</u>, where the number in the denominator is 1. The fraction bar can be read as "per".
>
> $$\frac{55 \text{ miles}}{1 \text{ hour}} = 55 \text{ miles per hour}$$

WORKED EXAMPLES

Find the unit rate for each problem. Write answers to the nearest tenth.

1. 140 mi to 4 in
    (scale on road map)

    $$\frac{140 \text{ mi}}{4 \text{ in}} \qquad 4\overline{)140}^{\,35}$$

    35 mi per in

2. 35 wood stoves built in 3 days

    $$\frac{35 \text{ stoves}}{3 \text{ days}} \qquad 3\overline{)35.00}^{\,11.66}$$

    11.7 stoves per day

3. 80 calories in 1.8 oz of eggs

    $$\frac{80 \text{ cal}}{1.8 \text{ oz}} \qquad 1.8\overline{)80.0.00}^{\,44.44}$$

    44.4 cal per oz

BRUSH-UP EXERCISES

1. 261 km in 3 hr

2. $1.65 for 6 cans of juice (How many cents per can?)

3. 4567 cars built in 11 weeks

SELF-CHECK ANSWERS

1. 87 km per hr   2. 27.5¢ per can   3. 415.2 cars per wk

ANSWERS

1. 10
2. 13
3. 18.5
4. 2.2
5. 0.9
6. 22.8

WORKED EXAMPLE

32 mi in 3 hr

$$3\overline{)32.00} = 10.66$$

Rounded to the nearest tenth,
the unit rate is 10.7 mi per hr.

Find a unit rate for each of the following.
Round each answer to the nearest tenth.

1. 100 m in 10 sec

unit rate: _____ m per sec

2. 65 calories in 5 min

unit rate: _____ cal per min

3. 388.5 mi on 21 gallons

unit rate: _____ mi per gallon (mpg)

4. 99 radios in 45 homes

unit rate: _____ radios per home

5. $27\frac{1}{2}$ lb in 30 days

unit rate: _____ lb per day

6. 364 students in 16 classes

unit rate: _____ students per class

466

<table>
<tr><td>

WORKED EXAMPLE

$43.20 earned in 8 hr

$$\begin{array}{r} 5.40 \\ 8\overline{)43.20} \end{array}$$

Unit rate: $5.40 per hr

</td></tr>
</table>

Find a unit rate for each of the following.

1. $272.00 earned in 40 hours

   unit rate: _____

2. $1500.00 of commissions in 12 months

   unit rate: _____

3. $980.00 earned in 4 weeks

   unit rate: _____

4. $2920.00 earned in 8 weeks

   unit rate: _____

5. $177.80 spent in 7 days

   unit rate: _____

6. $1022.00 spent in 4 weeks

   unit rate: _____

7. $1744.80 spent in 12 car installments

   unit rate: _____

8. $2073.60 in 24 installments

   unit rate: _____

9. $4257.60 spent in 12 home installments

   unit rate: _____

467

WORKED EXAMPLE

67.6 fluid oz in 2 L

$$2\overline{)67.6}^{33.8}$$

Unit rate: 33.8 fl oz per L

This is called a <u>conversion</u> rate.

Find a unit rate for each of the following. Round each answer to the nearest tenth.

1. 11.55 ft in 3.5 m

2. 38.1 cm in 15 inches

3. 19.3 km in 12 mi

4. 77.6 L in 20.5 gallons

5. 43.1 lb in 19.6 kg

6. 311.9 g in 11 oz

7. 31.8 quarts in 35 L (dry measure)

8. 24.6 mL in 5 teaspoons (fluid measure)

```
         WORKED EXAMPLE
          2220 m in 8 min
                277.5
           8)2220.0
          227.5 m per min
```

Find a unit rate for each of the following. Round each answer to the nearest tenth.

1. 4365 m in 20 min

2. 520 km in 8 hr

3. 307.8 km on 9 L

4. 488 km in 6 hr

5. 128 people on 2 buses

6. 672 cars inspected in 12 hr

7. 1752 trees planted by 5 foresters

8. 486 acres surveyed by 8 engineers

SKILL 1

1. $\dfrac{1}{3}$

2. $\dfrac{6}{1}$

3. $\dfrac{21}{4}$

4. $\dfrac{100}{3}$

5. $\dfrac{4}{15}$

6. $\dfrac{16}{9}$

SKILL 2

1. $\dfrac{25 \text{ m}}{3 \text{ sec}}$

2. $\dfrac{8 \text{ g}}{\$5}$

3. $\dfrac{2 \text{ runs}}{3 \text{ innings}}$

4. $\dfrac{3 \text{ teachers}}{80 \text{ students}}$

5. $\dfrac{52 \text{ mi}}{1 \text{ hr}}$

6. $\dfrac{2 \text{ g}}{\$5}$

SKILL 3

1. 2 gal per hr

2. 13 mi per in

3. 12.5 cal per hr

4. 25¢ per apple

5. 25.3 problems per hr

6. 23.9 mi per gal

SKILL 1   Write each ratio as a fraction in lowest terms.

1. 15 mi to 45 mi   2. 12 oz to 2 oz   3. 63 m to 12 m

4. 2 L to 60 mL   5. 56¢ to $2.10   6. 1 hr 20 min to 45 min

SKILL 2   Write each rate in simplest form, using a fraction.

1. 100 m in 12 sec   2. 24 g for $15   3. 6 runs in 9 innings

4. 6 teachers for 160 students   5. 260 mi in 5 hr   6. 8 g for $20

SKILL 3   Find the unit rate for each problem. Round to the nearest tenth or cent.

1. 18 g in 9 hr   2. 65 mi to 5 in   3. 150 calories in 12 hr

4. $4 for 16 apples   5. 76 problems in 3 hr   6. 167 mi on 7 gallons

PROPORTIONS

OBJECTIVE Skill 4 Determine if proportions are true.

SKILL MODEL

Is the proportion TRUE? $\frac{6}{8} \overset{?}{=} \frac{48}{64}$ **PROBLEM**	**THINK** If cross-products are equal, then the proportion is true. Find the two cross-products. $\frac{6}{8} \times \frac{48}{64}$ ⟹ 8×48 ⟹ 6×64	$6 \times 64 \overset{?}{=} 8 \times 48$ $384 = 384$ ⇧ Cross-products are equal.	The proportion $\frac{6}{8} = \frac{48}{64}$ is TRUE. **ANSWER**
	1	**2**	**3**

SOLUTION STEPS

Step 1 Find the cross-products of the ratios.

Step 2 Write the cross-products in an equation and determine if they are equal.

Step 3 The proportion is true since the cross-products are equal. Write the answer.

REMEMBER

A proportion is a statement that two ratios are equal. If the two cross-products are equal, then the ratios are equal. So the proportion is TRUE.

WORKED EXAMPLES

Tell if each proportion is TRUE (T) or NOT TRUE (NT).

1. $\frac{2}{3} \overset{?}{=} \frac{7}{12}$

$2 \times 12 \overset{?}{=} 3 \times 21$

$24 \overset{?}{=} 63$

$\boxed{\text{NT}}$

2. $\frac{24}{40} \overset{?}{=} \frac{144}{240}$

$24 \times 240 \overset{?}{=} 40 \times 144$

$5760 \overset{?}{=} 5760$

$\boxed{\text{T}}$

3. $\frac{3.2}{16} \overset{?}{=} \frac{2}{10}$

$3.2 \times 10 \overset{?}{=} 16 \times 2$

$32 \overset{?}{=} 32$

$\boxed{\text{T}}$

BRUSH-UP EXERCISES

1. $\frac{3}{4} \overset{?}{=} \frac{9}{8}$

2. $\frac{3}{8} \overset{?}{=} \frac{9}{24}$

3. $\frac{5}{8} \overset{?}{=} \frac{40}{88}$

4. $\frac{16}{8} \overset{?}{=} \frac{4}{20}$

5. $\frac{12}{86} \overset{?}{=} \frac{72}{516}$

6. $\frac{2}{450} \overset{?}{=} \frac{6}{1350}$

SELF-CHECK ANSWERS

1. NT   2. T   3. NT   4. NT   5. T   6. T

PRACTICE   PROPORTIONS   Skill 4

page 1

Complete. Tell if each proportion is TRUE (T) or NOT TRUE (NT).

ANSWERS

1. 1; 4; T
2. 6; 18; T
3. 2; 18; NT
4. 4; 24; T
5. 8; 8; T
6. 2; 18; NT
7. 8; 8; NT
8. 3; 3; NT
9. 3; 6; T
10. 8; 56; T
11. 12; 48; NT
12. 8; 64; NT
13. 12; 60; T
14. 6; 96; NT
15. 15; 30; NT

WORKED EXAMPLE

$$\frac{3}{4} \overset{?}{=} \frac{6}{8}$$
$$3 \times 8 \overset{?}{=} 4 \times 6$$
$$24 \overset{?}{=} 24$$
$$\boxed{T}$$

1. $\frac{1}{2} \overset{?}{=} \frac{2}{4}$

_____ $\times 4 \overset{?}{=} 2 \times 2$

_____ $\overset{?}{=} 4$

2. $\frac{2}{3} \overset{?}{=} \frac{6}{9}$

$2 \times 9 \overset{?}{=} 3 \times$ _____

$18 \overset{?}{=}$ _____

3. $\frac{2}{5} \overset{?}{=} \frac{4}{9}$

_____ $\times 9 \overset{?}{=} 5 \times 4$

_____ $\overset{?}{=} 20$

4. $\frac{3}{4} \overset{?}{=} \frac{6}{8}$

$3 \times 8 \overset{?}{=}$ _____ $\times 6$

$24 \overset{?}{=}$ _____

5. $\frac{1}{4} \overset{?}{=} \frac{2}{8}$

$1 \times$ _____ $\overset{?}{=} 4 \times 2$

_____ $\overset{?}{=} 8$

6. $\frac{2}{3} \overset{?}{=} \frac{4}{9}$

_____ $\times 9 \overset{?}{=} 3 \times 4$

_____ $\overset{?}{=} 12$

7. $\frac{1}{4} \overset{?}{=} \frac{3}{8}$

$1 \times$ _____ $\overset{?}{=} 4 \times 3$

_____ $\overset{?}{=} 12$

8. $\frac{2}{3} \overset{?}{=} \frac{1}{8}$

$2 \times 8 \overset{?}{=}$ _____ $\times 1$

$16 \overset{?}{=}$ _____

9. $\frac{1}{2} \overset{?}{=} \frac{3}{6}$

$1 \times 6 \overset{?}{=} 2 \times$ _____

$6 \overset{?}{=}$ _____

10. $\frac{4}{7} \overset{?}{=} \frac{8}{14}$

$4 \times 14 \overset{?}{=} 7 \times$ _____

$56 \overset{?}{=}$ _____

11. $\frac{4}{5} \overset{?}{=} \frac{8}{12}$

$4 \times$ _____ $\overset{?}{=} 5 \times 8$

_____ $\overset{?}{=} 40$

12. $\frac{5}{8} \overset{?}{=} \frac{8}{16}$

$5 \times 16 \overset{?}{=} 8 \times$ _____

$80 \overset{?}{=}$ _____

13. $\frac{4}{5} \overset{?}{=} \frac{12}{15}$

$4 \times 15 \overset{?}{=} 5 \times$ _____

$60 \overset{?}{=}$ _____

14. $\frac{16}{24} \overset{?}{=} \frac{1}{6}$

$16 \times$ _____ $\overset{?}{=} 24 \times 1$

_____ $\overset{?}{=} 24$

15. $\frac{10}{15} \overset{?}{=} \frac{2}{5}$

$10 \times 5 \overset{?}{=}$ _____ $\times 2$

$50 \overset{?}{=}$ _____

WORKED EXAMPLE

$$\frac{7}{9} \overset{?}{=} \frac{8}{12}$$

$$7 \times 12 \overset{?}{=} 9 \times 8$$

$$84 \overset{?}{=} 72$$

NT

Tell if each proportion is TRUE (T) or NOT TRUE (NT).

1. $\frac{1}{3} \overset{?}{=} \frac{3}{9}$

2. $\frac{1}{2} \overset{?}{=} \frac{7}{9}$ **3.** $\frac{2}{4} \overset{?}{=} \frac{6}{8}$ **4.** $\frac{2}{4} \overset{?}{=} \frac{4}{8}$

5. $\frac{2}{3} \overset{?}{=} \frac{2}{6}$ **6.** $\frac{3}{5} \overset{?}{=} \frac{6}{7}$ **7.** $\frac{1}{4} \overset{?}{=} \frac{2}{8}$

8. $\frac{1}{2} \overset{?}{=} \frac{4}{8}$ **9.** $\frac{2}{7} \overset{?}{=} \frac{2}{8}$ **10.** $\frac{3}{9} \overset{?}{=} \frac{16}{36}$

11. $\frac{4}{5} \overset{?}{=} \frac{8}{10}$ **12.** $\frac{3}{8} \overset{?}{=} \frac{9}{16}$ **13.** $\frac{2}{7} \overset{?}{=} \frac{6}{14}$

14. $\frac{2}{3} \overset{?}{=} \frac{12}{18}$ **15.** $\frac{4}{5} \overset{?}{=} \frac{12}{15}$ **16.** $\frac{6}{7} \overset{?}{=} \frac{20}{21}$

17. $\frac{4}{8} \overset{?}{=} \frac{16}{32}$ **18.** $\frac{3}{4} \overset{?}{=} \frac{15}{20}$ **19.** $\frac{3}{5} \overset{?}{=} \frac{40}{18}$

ANSWERS

1. T
2. NT
3. NT
4. T
5. NT
6. NT
7. T
8. T
9. NT
10. NT
11. T
12. NT
13. NT
14. T
15. T
16. NT
17. T
18. T
19. NT

Tell if each proportion is TRUE (T) or NOT TRUE (NT).

ANSWERS
1. NT
2. T
3. NT
4. T
5. NT
6. NT
7. NT
8. T
9. T
10. NT
11. T
12. T
13. T
14. NT
15. T
16. T
17. T
18. NT
19. T
20. T
21. NT

1. $\frac{4}{7} \stackrel{?}{=} \frac{2}{3}$

2. $\frac{6}{9} \stackrel{?}{=} \frac{2}{3}$

3. $\frac{4}{8} \stackrel{?}{=} \frac{1}{4}$

4. $\frac{3}{9} \stackrel{?}{=} \frac{1}{3}$

5. $\frac{4}{6} \stackrel{?}{=} \frac{1}{3}$

6. $\frac{7}{9} \stackrel{?}{=} \frac{1}{5}$

7. $\frac{7}{40} \stackrel{?}{=} \frac{7}{8}$

8. $\frac{6}{21} \stackrel{?}{=} \frac{2}{7}$

9. $\frac{8}{36} \stackrel{?}{=} \frac{2}{9}$

10. $\frac{40}{6} \stackrel{?}{=} \frac{8}{14}$

11. $\frac{24}{64} \stackrel{?}{=} \frac{6}{16}$

12. $\frac{18}{32} \stackrel{?}{=} \frac{9}{16}$

13. $\frac{12}{80} \stackrel{?}{=} \frac{3}{20}$

14. $\frac{14}{48} \stackrel{?}{=} \frac{5}{16}$

15. $\frac{12}{33} \stackrel{?}{=} \frac{4}{11}$

16. $\frac{8}{100} \stackrel{?}{=} \frac{2}{25}$

17. $\frac{6}{252} \stackrel{?}{=} \frac{1}{42}$

18. $\frac{4}{186} \stackrel{?}{=} \frac{3}{92}$

19. $\frac{3}{450} \stackrel{?}{=} \frac{6}{900}$

20. $\frac{1}{624} \stackrel{?}{=} \frac{5}{3120}$

21. $\frac{5}{4250} \stackrel{?}{=} \frac{1}{425}$

OBJECTIVE   Skill 5   Solve true proportions.

SKILL MODEL

PROBLEM

Solve the proportion

$$\frac{3}{8} = \frac{15}{m}$$

$m = ?$

1

$$\frac{3}{8} \bowtie \frac{15}{m} \Rightarrow \begin{matrix} 8 \times 15 \\ 3 \times m \end{matrix}$$

$$3 \times m = 8 \times 15$$

2

$$3 \times m = 8 \times 15$$

$$3 \times m = 120$$

$$\frac{\overset{1}{\cancel{3}} \times m}{\cancel{3}_1} = \frac{\overset{40}{\cancel{120}}}{\cancel{3}_1}$$

$$m = 40$$

3

$$m = 40$$

____ CHECK _____

$3 \times 40 \overset{?}{=} 8 \times 15$

$120 = 120$

The answer is correct.

_____ **ANSWER**

SOLUTION STEPS

Step 1   ''Solving'' a proportion means finding the number which makes the proportion TRUE. Begin by writing the cross-products in an equation.

Step 2   Solve the equation for m by dividing both sides by 3.

Step 3   Write the answer. Check your work by seeing if the answer gives equal cross-products.

> **NOTE**
> $$120 = 120$$
> $$\frac{120}{3} = \frac{120}{3}$$
> If an equation is true, and you divide both sides of the equation by the same number, then the resulting equation is also true.

WORKED EXAMPLES

Find the unknown value in each proportion.

1. $\frac{3}{4} = \frac{n}{12}$

     $3 \times 12 = 4 \times n$

     $\frac{36}{4} = n$

     $9 = n$

2. $\frac{28}{52} = \frac{s}{13}$

     $28 \times 13 = 52 \times s$

     $\frac{364}{52} = s$

     $7 = s$

3. $\frac{29}{1450} = \frac{6}{d}$

     $29 \times d = 1450 \times 6$

     $d = \frac{8700}{29}$

     $d = 300$

BRUSH-UP EXERCISES

1. $\frac{2}{3} = \frac{m}{36}$

2. $\frac{7}{n} = \frac{21}{81}$

3. $\frac{d}{46} = \frac{384}{552}$

     $m = $ _____

     $n = $ _____

     $d = $ _____

SELF-CHECK ANSWERS

1. 24   **2.** 27   **3.** 32

PRACTICE   PROPORTIONS   Skill 5

Find the unknown value in each proportion. Check the answer.

ANSWERS
1. 25
2. 49
3. 52
4. 5
5. 10
6. 12
7. 10
8. 4
9. 8
10. 2
11. 3
12. 1

WORKED EXAMPLE

$\frac{3}{4} = \frac{12}{m}$

$3 \times m = 4 \times 12$

$m = 16$

CHECK

$3 \times 16 \overset{?}{=} 4 \times 12$

$48 = 48$

answer checks

1. $\frac{2}{5} = \frac{10}{m}$

$m = $ _____

2. $\frac{2}{7} = \frac{14}{c}$

$c = $ _____

3. $\frac{1}{4} = \frac{13}{b}$

$b = $ _____

4. $\frac{3}{6} = \frac{a}{10}$

$a = $ _____

5. $\frac{4}{6} = \frac{m}{15}$

$m = $ _____

6. $\frac{2}{3} = \frac{b}{18}$

$b = $ _____

7. $\frac{3}{n} = \frac{12}{40}$

$n = $ _____

8. $\frac{2}{a} = \frac{10}{20}$

$a = $ _____

9. $\frac{6}{z} = \frac{15}{20}$

$z = $ _____

10. $\frac{a}{8} = \frac{6}{24}$

$a = $ _____

11. $\frac{c}{6} = \frac{12}{24}$

$c = $ _____

12. $\frac{a}{3} = \frac{10}{30}$

$a = $ _____

PRACTICE

PROPORTIONS

Skill 5

$$\frac{4}{16} = \frac{a}{12}$$

$$4 \times 12 = 16 \times a$$

$$a = 3$$

CHECK

$$4 \times 12 \overset{?}{=} 16 \times 3$$

$$48 = 48$$

answer checks

Find the unknown value in each proportion. Check the answer.

ANSWERS

1. 30
2. 30
3. 30
4. 5
5. 9
6. 5
7. 6
8. 8
9. 9
10. 2
11. 2
12. 1

1. $\frac{3}{6} = \frac{15}{b}$

$b = $ _____

2. $\frac{2}{3} = \frac{20}{c}$

$c = $ _____

3. $\frac{3}{9} = \frac{10}{d}$

$d = $ _____

4. $\frac{4}{8} = \frac{m}{10}$

$m = $ _____

5. $\frac{3}{4} = \frac{z}{12}$

$z = $ _____

6. $\frac{6}{12} = \frac{n}{10}$

$n = $ _____

7. $\frac{4}{b} = \frac{8}{12}$

$b = $ _____

8. $\frac{6}{m} = \frac{12}{16}$

$m = $ _____

9. $\frac{3}{a} = \frac{10}{30}$

$a = $ _____

10. $\frac{z}{4} = \frac{12}{24}$

$z = $ _____

11. $\frac{a}{3} = \frac{10}{15}$

$a = $ _____

12. $\frac{m}{6} = \frac{5}{30}$

$m = $ _____

ANSWERS
1. 3
2. 5
3. 8
4. 185
5. 330
6. 5
7. 210
8. 1
9. 331
10. 30
11. 620
12. 2575
13. 3

WORKED EXAMPLE

$$\frac{7}{54} = \frac{n}{270}$$

$$7 \times 270 = 54 \times n$$

$$35 = n$$

CHECK

$$7 \times 270 \overset{?}{=} 54 \times 35$$

$$1890 = 1890$$

answer checks

Find the unknown value in each proportion. Check the answer.

1. $\frac{5}{260} = \frac{m}{156}$

$m = $ _____

2. $\frac{1}{68} = \frac{z}{340}$

$z = $ _____

3. $\frac{1}{84} = \frac{b}{672}$

$b = $ _____

4. $\frac{14}{370} = \frac{7}{m}$

$m = $ _____

5. $\frac{3}{198} = \frac{5}{n}$

$n = $ _____

6. $\frac{8}{808} = \frac{a}{505}$

$a = $ _____

7. $\frac{5}{350} = \frac{3}{s}$

$s = $ _____

8. $\frac{4}{1240} = \frac{m}{310}$

$m = $ _____

9. $\frac{5}{1655} = \frac{1}{a}$

$a = $ _____

10. $\frac{b}{165} = \frac{2}{11}$

$b = $ _____

11. $\frac{1}{s} = \frac{3}{1860}$

$s = $ _____

12. $\frac{5}{m} = \frac{6}{3090}$

$m = $ _____

13. $\frac{a}{2193} = \frac{5}{3655}$

$a = $ _____

OBJECTIVE   Skill 6   Write equal rates as a proportion, then solve.

SKILL MODEL

30 sales in 5 days = m sales in 20 days

Write as a proportion, then solve.

PROBLEM

$$\frac{30 \text{ sales}}{5 \text{ days}} = \frac{m \text{ sales}}{20 \text{ days}}$$

$$\frac{30}{5} = \frac{m}{20}$$

$$600 = 5m$$

$$120 = m$$

1 & 2

$m = 120$

The corresponding rate is

120 sales in 20 days

ANSWER

3

SOLUTION STEPS

Step 1   Set the known rate equal to the rate with the unknown value.

Step 2   Write a proportion using only the number parts of the rates, then solve.

Step 3   Write the answer and use it to express the corresponding rate.

REMEMBER

In writing equal rates as a proportion, make sure both numerators have the same units (sales), and both denominators have the same units (days).

WORKED EXAMPLES

1. 150 campers on 6 acres = s campers on 10 acres

$$\frac{150}{6} = \frac{s}{10}$$

$$1500 = 6 \times s$$

$$250 = s$$

250 campers on 10 acres

2. 2 km walked in 50 min = n km walked in $2\frac{1}{2}$ hr

($2\frac{1}{2}$ hr = 150 min)

$$\frac{2}{50} = \frac{n}{150}$$

$$300 = 50 \times n$$

$$6 = n$$

6 km walked in $2\frac{1}{2}$ hr

BRUSH-UP EXERCISES

Solve for the unknown and write the corresponding rate.

1. 48 pages typed in 16 hr = 144 pages typed in x hr

2. 4 km walked in 50 min = s km walked in 1 hr 40 min

3. t dollars earned in 3 months = \$2458 earned in 4 months

SELF-CHECK ANSWERS

1. $x = 48$; 144 pages in 48 hr   2. $s = 8$; 8 km in 1 hr 40 min   3. $t = 1843.5$; \$1843.50 in 3 mo

Copyright © 1980 by Houghton Mifflin Company. All rights reserved.

ANSWERS

1. $\dfrac{40}{18.60} = \dfrac{s}{56.80}$

2. $\dfrac{10}{7.00} = \dfrac{t}{140.00}$

3. $\dfrac{4}{80} = \dfrac{s}{400}$

4. $\dfrac{4}{80} = \dfrac{1}{t}$

5. $\dfrac{50}{15.00} = \dfrac{5}{y}$

6. $\dfrac{20}{6.20} = \dfrac{n}{3.10}$

7. $\dfrac{20}{6.20} = \dfrac{1}{t}$

8. $\dfrac{1}{12.50} = \dfrac{x}{37.50}$

9. $\dfrac{2}{428.00} = \dfrac{m}{856.00}$

10. $\dfrac{12}{18.00} = \dfrac{48}{s}$

11. $\dfrac{m}{14.00} = \dfrac{10}{65.00}$

12. $\dfrac{x}{24.50} = \dfrac{6}{75.00}$

13. $\dfrac{s}{125.00} = \dfrac{3}{375.00}$

14. $\dfrac{m}{450.00} = \dfrac{8}{1,800.00}$

15. $\dfrac{4}{t} = \dfrac{10}{220.00}$

WORKED EXAMPLE

50 kg for \$27.50 = n kg for \$55.00

$$\dfrac{50}{27.50} = \dfrac{n}{55.00}$$

Write each pair of rates as a proportion. DO NOT SOLVE.

Equal Rates	Proportion
1. 40 kg for \$18.60 = s kg for \$56.80	
2. 10 kg for \$7.00 = t kg for \$140.00	
3. 4 kg for 80¢ = s kg for \$4.00	
4. 4 kg for 80¢ = 1 kg for t cents	
5. 50 kg for \$15.00 = 5 kg for y dollars	
6. 20 kg for \$6.20 = n kg for \$3.10	
7. 20 kg for \$6.20 = 1 kg for t dollars	
8. 1 shirt for \$12.50 = x shirts for \$37.50	
9. 2 suits for \$428.00 = m suits for \$856.00	
10. 12 golf balls for \$18.00 = 48 golf balls for s dollars	
11. m games for \$14.00 = 10 games for \$65.00	
12. x meals for \$24.50 = 6 meals for \$75.00	
13. s car repairs for \$125.00 = 3 car repairs for \$375.00	
14. m trips for \$450.00 = 8 trips for \$1,800.00	
15. 4 gifts for t dollars = 10 gifts for \$220.00	

PRACTICE

PROPORTIONS

WORKED EXAMPLE

60 people in 2 shuttles
t people in 8 shuttles

$$\frac{60}{2} = \frac{t}{8}$$
$$t = 240$$

rate: 240 people in 8 shuttles

Write each proportion. Solve for the unknown and write the corresponding rate.

A. Auditorium capacity: 120 people in 2 rows.

1. n people in 10 rows

$n =$ _____

rate: _____

2. t people in 20 rows

$t =$ _____

rate: _____

3. s people in 40 rows

$s =$ _____

rate: _____

4. m people in 60 rows

$m =$ _____

rate: _____

5. 600 people in x rows

$x =$ _____

rate: _____

6. 1800 people in y rows

$y =$ _____

rate: _____

B. km walked: 1 km in 15 min

7. x km in 45 min

$x =$ _____

rate: _____

8. t km in 60 min

$t =$ _____

rate: _____

9. 10 km in s min

$s =$ _____

rate: _____

10. 20 km in z min

$z =$ _____

rate: _____

1. $\frac{120}{2} = \frac{n}{10}$; $n = 600$; 600 people in 10 rows

2. $\frac{120}{2} = \frac{t}{20}$; $t = 1200$; 1200 people in 20 rows

3. $\frac{120}{2} = \frac{s}{40}$; $s = 2400$; 2400 people in 40 rows

4. $\frac{120}{2} = \frac{m}{60}$; $m = 3600$; 3600 people in 60 rows

5. $\frac{120}{2} = \frac{600}{x}$; $x = 10$; 600 people in 10 rows

6. $\frac{120}{2} = \frac{1800}{y}$; $y = 30$; 1800 people in 30 rows

7. $\frac{1}{15} = \frac{x}{45}$; $x = 3$; 3 km in 45 min

8. $\frac{1}{15} = \frac{t}{60}$; $t = 4$; 4 km in 60 min

9. $\frac{1}{15} = \frac{10}{s}$; $s = 150$; 10 km in 150 min

10. $\frac{1}{15} = \frac{20}{z}$; $z = 300$; 20 km in 300 min

481

Write each proportion. Solve for the unknown and write the corresponding rate.

A. Air filter production: 1440 in 8 hr

1. s filters in 1 hr

$s =$ _____

rate: _____

2. t filters in 2 hr

$t =$ _____

rate: _____

3. m filters in 16 hr

$m =$ _____

rate: _____

4. y filters in 40 hr

$y =$ _____

rate: _____

5. 5760 filters in x hr

$x =$ _____

rate: _____

6. 34,560 filters in t hr

$t =$ _____

rate: _____

B. **7.** 725 km in 1 day $= t$ km in 2 days

$t =$ _____

rate: _____

8. 34 km on 1 L $= x$ km on 12 L

$x =$ _____

rate: _____

9. x m in 10 sec $=$ 500 m in 50 sec

$x =$ _____

rate: _____

10. 10 kg for \$3.80 $= s$ kg for \$30.40

$s =$ _____

rate: _____

ANSWERS

1. $\frac{1440}{8} = \frac{s}{1}$;
$s = 180$;
180 filters
in 1 hr

2. $\frac{1440}{8} = \frac{t}{2}$;
$t = 360$;
360 filters
in 2 hr

3. $\frac{1440}{8} = \frac{m}{16}$;
$m = 2880$;
2880 filters
in 16 hr

4. $\frac{1440}{8} = \frac{y}{40}$;
$y = 7200$;
7200 filters
in 40 hr

5. $\frac{1440}{8} = \frac{5760}{x}$;
$x = 32$;
5760 filters
in 32 hr

6. $\frac{1440}{8} = \frac{34,560}{t}$;
$t = 192$;
34,560 filters
in 192 hr

7. $\frac{725}{1} = \frac{t}{2}$;
$t = 1450$;
1450 km
in 2 days

8. $\frac{34}{1} = \frac{x}{12}$;
$x = 408$;
408 km on
12 L

9. $\frac{x}{10} = \frac{500}{50}$;
$x = 100$;
100 m in
10 sec

10. $\frac{10}{3.80} = \frac{s}{30.40}$;
$s = 80$;
80 kg for
\$30.40

Write each proportion. Solve for the unknown and write the corresponding rate.

1. 1600 m in 4 minutes = s m in 30 minutes

$s =$ _____

rate: _____

2. 2400 chips in 3 days = n chips in 5 days

$n =$ _____

rate: _____

3. 288 sq in for 1 table = 3456 sq in for x tables

$x =$ _____

rate: _____

4. 216 bricks in 2 walls = 1728 bricks in t walls

$t =$ _____

rate: _____

5. 64 cars in 8 min = 1024 cars in s min

$s =$ _____

rate: _____

6. 10 lunches for $24.80 = 40 lunches for t dollars

$t =$ _____

rate: _____

7. 5 days for $3.75 = 20 days for x dollars

$x =$ _____

rate: _____

8. x dollars for 1 suit = $384.00 for 3 suits

$x =$ _____

rate: _____

9. t dollars earned in 8 hr = $232.00 earned in 40 hr

$t =$ _____

rate: _____

ANSWERS

1. $\dfrac{1600}{4} = \dfrac{s}{30}$;
$s = 12,000$;
12,000 m
in 30 min

2. $\dfrac{2400}{3} = \dfrac{n}{5}$;
$n = 4000$;
4000 chips
in 5 days

3. $\dfrac{288}{1} = \dfrac{3456}{x}$;
$x = 12$;
3456 sq in
for 12 tables

4. $\dfrac{216}{2} = \dfrac{1728}{t}$;
$t = 16$;
1728 bricks
in 16 walls

5. $\dfrac{64}{8} = \dfrac{1024}{s}$;
$s = 128$;
1024 cars
in 128 min

6. $\dfrac{10}{24.80} = \dfrac{40}{t}$;
$t = 99.20$;
40 lunches
for $99.20

7. $\dfrac{5}{3.75} = \dfrac{20}{x}$;
$x = 15.00$;
20 days for
$15.00

8. $\dfrac{x}{1} = \dfrac{384.00}{3}$;
$x = 128.00$;
$128.00 for
1 suit

9. $\dfrac{t}{8} = \dfrac{232.00}{40}$;
$t = 46.40$;
$46.40 earned
in 8 hr

REVIEW
PROPORTIONS

SKILL 4

1. T

2. NT

3. T

4. NT

5. T

6. T

SKILL 4   Tell if each proportion is TRUE (T) or NOT TRUE (NT).

1. $\frac{3}{5} \overset{?}{=} \frac{6}{10}$　　**2.** $\frac{5}{9} \overset{?}{=} \frac{30}{45}$　　**3.** $\frac{1}{20} \overset{?}{=} \frac{3}{60}$

4. $\frac{6}{72} \overset{?}{=} \frac{2}{21}$　　**5.** $\frac{12}{108} \overset{?}{=} \frac{16}{144}$　　**6.** $\frac{24}{420} \overset{?}{=} \frac{16.8}{294}$

SKILL 5

1. 6

2. 12

3. 92

4. 3

5. 20

6. 12

SKILL 5   Find the unknown value in each proportion. Check the answer.

1. $\frac{2}{5} = \frac{d}{15}$　　**2.** $\frac{3}{8} = \frac{m}{32}$　　**3.** $\frac{69}{276} = \frac{23}{n}$

$d = $ _____　　$m = $ _____　　$n = $ _____

4. $\frac{s}{5} = \frac{84}{140}$　　**5.** $\frac{1}{t} = \frac{17}{340}$　　**6.** $\frac{n}{13} = \frac{1260}{1365}$

$s = $ _____　　$t = $ _____　　$n = $ _____

SKILL 6

1. $\frac{1400}{6} = \frac{m}{3}$;
$m = 700$;
700 tickets
sold in 3 days

2. $\frac{581}{t} = \frac{996}{12}$;
$t = 7$; 581 km
in 7 hr

3. $\frac{n}{5} = \frac{900}{8}$;
$n = 562.50$;
$562.50 saved
in 5 mo

SKILL 6   Write each proportion. Solve for the unknown and write the corresponding rate.

1. 1400 tickets sold in 6 days = m tickets sold in 3 days

2. 581 km traveled in t hr = 996 km traveled in 12 hr

3. n dollars saved in 5 mo = $900 saved in 8 mo

$m = $ _____　　$t = $ _____　　$n = $ _____

rate: _____　　rate: _____　　rate: _____

PROPORTIONS
Unit Mastery Test – Page 1
Answers on Page 542

SKILL 1   Write each ratio as a fraction in simplest form.

1. 80 kg to 30 kg   **2.** 64 oz to 24 oz   **3.** 2 ft 4 in to 10 in

SKILL 1

1.

2.

3.

SKILL 2   Write each rate in simplest form, using a fraction.

1. 32 mi in 5 hr   **2.** 80 km on 15 L   **3.** $1365 for 140 hr

SKILL 2

1.

2.

3.

SKILL 3   Find the unit rate for each problem. Round to the nearest tenth or cent.

1. 96¢ for 6 lemons   **2.** 64 mi in 6 hr   **3.** $390 for 12 weeks

SKILL 3

1.

2.

3.

Unit Mastery Test – Page 2

Answers on Page 542

SKILL 4

1.

2.

3.

SKILL 4 Tell if each proportion is TRUE (T) or NOT TRUE (NT).

1. $\dfrac{5}{9} \overset{?}{=} \dfrac{30}{54}$

2. $\dfrac{14}{16} \overset{?}{=} \dfrac{22}{64}$

3. $\dfrac{20}{32} \overset{?}{=} \dfrac{640}{704}$

SKILL 5

1.

2.

3.

SKILL 5 Find the unknown value in each proportion. Check the answer.

1. $\dfrac{5}{6} = \dfrac{m}{78}$

2. $\dfrac{d}{32} = \dfrac{264}{352}$

3. $\dfrac{1}{s} = \dfrac{5}{2150}$

$m = \underline{\hspace{1cm}}$ $d = \underline{\hspace{1cm}}$ $s = \underline{\hspace{1cm}}$

SKILL 6

1.

2.

3.

SKILL 6 Write each proportion. Solve for the unknown and write the corresponding rate.

1. 76 km on 2 L = s km on 6 L

2. 240 people in 3 subway cars = 720 people in m cars

3. n dollars saved in 8 months = $1,260 saved in 3 months

$s = \underline{\hspace{1cm}}$ $x = \underline{\hspace{1cm}}$ $t = \underline{\hspace{1cm}}$

rate: $\underline{\hspace{1.5cm}}$ rate: $\underline{\hspace{1.5cm}}$ rate: $\underline{\hspace{1.5cm}}$

UNIT 12
PERCENTS

Skill 1   Rewrite whole number percents up to 100%
                     in fractional or decimal form.

Skill 2   Rewrite whole number percents larger than 100%
                     in fractional or decimal form.

Skill 3   Rewrite percents less than 1%
                     in fractional or decimal form.

Skill 4   Rewrite mixed number and decimal percents
                     in fractional or decimal form.

Skill 5   Rewrite decimals as percents.

Skill 6   Rewrite fractions as percents.

Skill 7   Rewrite whole numbers and mixed numbers
                     as percents.

Skill 8   Find a percentage of a given number.

Skill 9   Find what percent one number is of another number.

Skill 10   Find a number if a percentage of the number
                     is known.

PERCENTS
Unit Diagnostic Test – Page 1
Answers on Page 541

SKILL 1 Write each percent in fractional and decimal form. Write fractional answers in lowest terms.

1. 7%   **2.** 50%   **3.** 64%

SKILL 2 Write each percent in fractional and decimal form. Write fractional answers in lowest terms.

1. 217%   **2.** 300%   **3.** 580%

SKILL 3 Write each percent in fractional and decimal form. Write fractional answers in lowest terms.

1. 0.65%   **2.** $\frac{1}{6}$%   **3.** $\frac{4}{5}$%

SKILL 4 Write each percent in fractional and decimal form. Write fractional answers in lowest terms. Round decimal answers as needed.

1. 71.25%   **2.** $65\frac{5}{8}$%   **3.** $213\frac{1}{3}$%

SKILL 5 Write each decimal as a percent. Write fractional answers in lowest terms.

1. 0.08   **2.** 0.232   **3.** 3.007

SKILL 1

1.

2.

3.

SKILL 2

1.

2.

3.

SKILL 3

1.

2.

3.

SKILL 4

1.

2.

3.

SKILL 5

1.

2.

3.

489

SKILL 6

1.

2.

3.

SKILL 6 Write each fraction as a percent. Write fractional answers in lowest terms. Round decimal answers as needed.

1. $\frac{1}{10}$
2. $\frac{3}{4}$
3. $\frac{4}{9}$

SKILL 7

1.

2.

3.

SKILL 7 Write each number as a percent. Write fractional answers in lowest terms. Round decimal answers as needed.

1. $5\frac{1}{2}$
2. $4\frac{7}{8}$
3. $2\frac{2}{3}$

SKILL 8

1.

2.

3.

SKILL 8

1. 3% of 160 is what number?
2. What is 110% of 150?
3. Find $6\frac{1}{4}$% of $500.

SKILL 9

1.

2.

3.

SKILL 9

1. What percent of 50 is 31?
2. $258 is what percent of $150?
3. What percent of 96 is 21.6?

SKILL 10

1.

2.

3.

SKILL 10

1. 16% of what number is 4?
2. 82 is 205% of what number?
3. 87.5% of what number is 42?

OBJECTIVE   Skill 1   Rewrite whole number percents up to 100% in fractional or decimal form.

SKILL MODEL

Write 75% in fractional form.

PROBLEM

Write 75% in decimal form.

$75\% = 75 \times \dfrac{1}{100} = \dfrac{75}{100}$

$75\% = 75 \times 0.01 = 0.75$

1

$75\% = \dfrac{75}{100} = \dfrac{3}{4}$

$75\% = 0.75$

ANSWER

2

SOLUTION STEPS

Step 1   Percent means hundredths: multiply 75 by one hundredth.
To get a fractional answer, multiply by one hundredth in the form $\dfrac{1}{100}$.
To get a decimal answer, multiply by one hundredth in the form 0.01

Step 2   Write the answers. Fractional answers should be written in lowest terms.

> **NOTE**
>
> Many applied problems involve percents. To solve these problems, percents must first be rewritten as fractions or decimals.

WORKED EXAMPLES

1. Write 3% in fractional and decimal form.

$3\% = 3 \times \dfrac{1}{100} = \dfrac{3}{100}$

$3\% = 3 \times 0.01 = 0.03$

2. Write 100% in fractional and decimal form.

$100\% = 100 \times \dfrac{1}{100} = 1$

$100\% = 100 \times 0.01 = 1$

3. Write 84% in fractional and decimal form.

$84\% = 84 \times \dfrac{1}{100} = \dfrac{84}{100}$

$\qquad\qquad = \dfrac{21}{25}$

$84\% = 84 \times 0.01 = 0.84$

BRUSH-UP EXERCISES

Write each percent in fractional and decimal form. Write fractional answers in lowest terms.

1. 7%   **2.** 4%   **3.** 50%

4. 27%   **5.** 65%   **6.** 82%

SELF-CHECK ANSWERS

1. $\dfrac{7}{100}$; 0.07   **2.** $\dfrac{1}{25}$; 0.04   **3.** $\dfrac{1}{2}$; 0.5   **4.** $\dfrac{27}{100}$; 0.27   **5.** $\dfrac{13}{20}$; 0.65   **6.** $\dfrac{41}{50}$; 0.82

Complete the following chart. Write each percent in fractional and decimal form. Write fractional answers in lowest terms.

ANSWERS

1. $\frac{9}{100}$; 0.09

2. $\frac{1}{20}$; 0.05

3. $\frac{2}{25}$; 0.08

4. $\frac{17}{100}$; 0.17

5. $\frac{1}{4}$; 0.25

6. $\frac{3}{10}$; 0.3

7. $\frac{43}{100}$; 0.43

8. $\frac{13}{25}$; 0.52

9. $\frac{13}{20}$; 0.65

10. $\frac{19}{25}$; 0.76

11. $\frac{87}{100}$; 0.87

12. $\frac{7}{10}$; 0.7

13. $\frac{31}{50}$; 0.62

14. $\frac{17}{20}$; 0.85

15. $\frac{24}{25}$; 0.96

16. $\frac{99}{100}$; 0.99

		Fractional Form	Decimal Form
1.	9%		
2.	5%		
3.	8%		
4.	17%		
5.	25%		
6.	30%		
7.	43%		
8.	52%		
9.	65%		
10.	76%		
11.	87%		
12.	70%		
13.	62%		
14.	85%		
15.	96%		
16.	99%		

LESSON PERCENTS Skill 2

OBJECTIVE   Skill 2   Rewrite whole number percents larger than 100% in fractional or decimal form.

SKILL MODEL

Write 350% in fractional form.

$$350\% = 350 \times \frac{1}{100} = \frac{350}{100}$$

$$350\% = \frac{350}{100} = 3\frac{1}{2}$$

Write 350% in decimal form.

PROBLEM

$$350\% = 350 \times 0.01 = 3.5$$

$$350\% = 3.5$$

ANSWER

1 **2**

SOLUTION STEPS

Step 1   Percent means hundredths: multiply 350 by one hundredth.
To get a fractional answer, multiply by one hundredth in the form $\frac{1}{100}$.
To get a decimal answer, multiply by one hundredth in the form 0.01

Step 2   Write the answers. Fractional answers should be written in lowest terms.

A SHORT CUT
To change a percent to a decimal, simply move the decimal point two places to the <u>left</u>.
$$350\% = 3.50. = 3.50$$

REMEMBER
Percents larger than 100% represent numbers larger than 1.
$$100\% = 1$$
$$350\% = 3.5 \text{ or } 3\frac{1}{2}$$

WORKED EXAMPLES

1. Write 119% in fractional and decimal form.

$$119\% = 119 \times \frac{1}{100}$$
$$= \frac{119}{100} = 1\frac{19}{100}$$
$$119\% = 119 \times 0.01 = 1.19$$

2. Write 200% in fractional and decimal form.

$$200\% = 200 \times \frac{1}{100}$$
$$= \frac{200}{100} = 2$$
$$200\% = 200 \times 0.01 = 2$$

3. Write 485% in fractional and decimal form.

$$485\% = 485 \times \frac{1}{100} = \frac{485}{100}$$
$$= 4\frac{17}{20}$$
$$485\% = 485 \times 0.01 = 4.85$$

BRUSH-UP EXERCISES

Write each percent in fractional and decimal form.

1. 103%   **2.** 170%   **3.** 500%

4. 150%   **5.** 425%   **6.** 240%

SELF-CHECK ANSWERS

1. $1\frac{3}{100}$; 1.03   **2.** $1\frac{7}{10}$; 1.7   **3.** 5; 5   **4.** $1\frac{1}{2}$; 1.5   **5.** $4\frac{1}{4}$; 4.25   **6.** $2\frac{2}{5}$; 2.4

493

ANSWERS

1. $1\frac{31}{100}$; 1.31

2. $1\frac{73}{100}$; 1.73

3. 3; 3

4. $2\frac{47}{100}$; 2.47

5. $2\frac{33}{100}$; 2.33

6. $3\frac{19}{100}$; 3.19

7. $1\frac{7}{100}$; 1.07

8. 4; 4

9. $3\frac{41}{100}$; 3.41

10. $4\frac{1}{100}$; 4.01

11. $4\frac{27}{100}$; 4.27

12. $5\frac{59}{100}$; 5.59

13. $4\frac{11}{100}$; 4.11

14. $6\frac{63}{100}$; 6.63

15. $4\frac{39}{100}$; 4.39

16. $5\frac{7}{100}$; 5.07

17. 6; 6

18. $3\frac{69}{100}$; 3.69

19. $4\frac{51}{100}$; 4.51

20. $5\frac{77}{100}$; 5.77

21. $6\frac{19}{100}$; 6.19

22. $4\frac{43}{100}$; 4.43

WORKED EXAMPLE

$$127\% = 127 \times \frac{1}{100} = \frac{127}{100}$$
$$= 1\frac{27}{100}$$

$$127\% = 127 \times 0.01 = 1.27$$

Write each percent in fractional and decimal form.

1. 131%

2. 173%

3. 300%

4. 247%

5. 233%

6. 319%

7. 107%

8. 400%

9. 341%

10. 401%

11. 427%

12. 559%

13. 411%

14. 663%

15. 439%

16. 507%

17. 600%

18. 369%

19. 451%

20. 577%

21. 619%

22. 443%

WORKED EXAMPLE
$475\% = 475 \times \dfrac{1}{100} = \dfrac{475}{100} = 4\dfrac{75}{100}$
$= 4\dfrac{3}{4}$
$475\% = 475 \times 0.01 = 4.75$

Write each percent in fractional and decimal form. Write fractional answers in lowest terms.

1. 125%

2. 240%

3. 250%

4. 130%

5. 320%

6. 270%

7. 115%

8. 280%

9. 390%

10. 235%

11. 224%

12. 420%

13. 375%

14. 314%

15. 405%

16. 520%

17. 450%

18. 206%

19. 530%

20. 325%

21. 512%

22. 460%

23. 770%

24. 605%

ANSWERS

1. $1\dfrac{1}{4}$; 1.25

2. $2\dfrac{2}{5}$; 2.4

3. $2\dfrac{1}{2}$; 2.5

4. $1\dfrac{3}{10}$; 1.3

5. $3\dfrac{1}{5}$; 3.2

6. $2\dfrac{7}{10}$; 2.7

7. $1\dfrac{3}{20}$; 1.15

8. $2\dfrac{4}{5}$; 2.8

9. $3\dfrac{9}{10}$; 3.9

10. $2\dfrac{7}{20}$; 2.35

11. $2\dfrac{6}{25}$; 2.24

12. $4\dfrac{1}{5}$; 4.2

13. $3\dfrac{3}{4}$; 3.75

14. $3\dfrac{7}{50}$; 3.14

15. $4\dfrac{1}{20}$; 4.05

16. $5\dfrac{1}{5}$; 5.2

17. $4\dfrac{1}{2}$; 4.5

18. $2\dfrac{3}{50}$; 2.06

19. $5\dfrac{3}{10}$; 5.3

20. $3\dfrac{1}{4}$; 3.25

21. $5\dfrac{3}{25}$; 5.12

22. $4\dfrac{3}{5}$; 4.6

23. $7\dfrac{7}{10}$; 7.7

24. $6\dfrac{1}{20}$; 6.05

Complete the following chart. Write each percent in fractional and decimal form. Write fractional answers in lowest terms.

		Fractional Form	Decimal Form
1.	117%		
2.	150%		
3.	215%		
4.	290%		
5.	300%		
6.	212%		
7.	225%		
8.	365%		
9.	409%		
10.	560%		
11.	400%		
12.	510%		
13.	575%		
14.	464%		
15.	306%		
16.	680%		

OBJECTIVE Skill 3 Rewrite percents less than 1% in fractional or decimal form.

SKILL MODEL

Write $\frac{1}{2}$% in fractional form.

Write $\frac{1}{2}$% in decimal form.

PROBLEM

$\frac{1}{2}$% $= \frac{1}{2} \times \frac{1}{100} = \frac{1}{200}$

$\frac{1}{2}$% $= \frac{1}{2} \times 0.01 = 0.5 \times 0.01 = 0.005$

1

$\frac{1}{2}$% $= \frac{1}{200}$

$\frac{1}{2}$% $= 0.005$

ANSWER

2

SOLUTION STEPS

Step 1 Percent means hundredths: multiply $\frac{1}{2}$ by one hundredth.
To get a fractional answer, multiply by one hundredth in the form $\frac{1}{100}$.
To get a decimal answer, multiply by one hundredth in the form 0.01

Step 2 Write the answers. Fractional answers should be written in lowest terms.

> **NOTE**
>
> If a decimal does not terminate by the ten-thousandths place, round to the nearest thousandth.
>
> $\frac{5}{12} = 12\overline{)5.0000}^{\,0.4166} \doteq 0.417$

WORKED EXAMPLES

1. Write 0.3% as a fraction and as a decimal.

$0.3\% = \frac{3}{10} \times \frac{1}{100} = \frac{3}{1000}$
$0.3\% = 0.3 \times 0.01$
$\quad\quad = 0.003$

2. Write 0.85% as a fraction and as a decimal.

$0.85\% = \frac{85}{100} \times \frac{1}{100}$
$\quad\quad = \frac{85}{10,000} = \frac{17}{2000}$
$0.85\% = 0.85 \times 0.01$
$\quad\quad = 0.0085$

3. Write $\frac{2}{3}$% as a fraction and as a decimal.

$\frac{2}{3}\% = \frac{2}{3} \times \frac{1}{100} = \frac{2}{300}$
$\quad\quad = \frac{1}{150}$
$\frac{2}{3}\% \doteq 0.667 \times 0.01$
$\quad\quad = 0.00667$

BRUSH-UP EXERCISES

Write each percent in fractional and decimal form. Write fractional answers in lowest terms. Round decimal answers as needed.

1. 0.7%

2. 0.66%

3. 0.75%

4. $\frac{2}{5}$%

5. $\frac{1}{8}$%

6. $\frac{5}{6}$%

SELF-CHECK ANSWERS

1. $\frac{7}{1000}$; 0.007 **2.** $\frac{33}{5000}$; 0.0066 **3.** $\frac{3}{400}$; 0.0075 **4.** $\frac{1}{250}$; 0.004

5. $\frac{1}{800}$; 0.00125 **6.** $\frac{1}{120}$; $\doteq 0.00833$

ANSWERS

1. $\frac{9}{1000}$; 0.009

2. $\frac{17}{10,000}$; 0.0017

3. $\frac{1}{400}$; 0.0025

4. $\frac{39}{10,000}$; 0.0039

5. $\frac{1}{200}$; 0.005

6. $\frac{2}{625}$; 0.0032

7. $\frac{13}{2500}$; 0.0052

8. $\frac{9}{2000}$; 0.0045

9. $\frac{29}{5000}$; 0.0058

10. $\frac{13}{2000}$; 0.0065

11. $\frac{1}{125}$; 0.008

12. $\frac{19}{2500}$; 0.0076

13. $\frac{83}{10,000}$; 0.0083

14. $\frac{7}{1000}$; 0.007

15. $\frac{31}{5000}$; 0.0062

16. $\frac{3}{400}$; 0.0075

17. $\frac{3}{2000}$; 0.0015

18. $\frac{71}{10,000}$; 0.0071

19. $\frac{3}{500}$; 0.006

20. $\frac{19}{2000}$; 0.0095

21. $\frac{9}{1250}$; 0.0072

22. $\frac{47}{5000}$; 0.0094

WORKED EXAMPLE

$$0.35\% = \frac{35}{100} \times \frac{1}{100} = \frac{35}{10,000}$$
$$= \frac{7}{2000}$$

$$0.35\% = 0.35 \times 0.01$$
$$= 0.0035$$

Write each percent in fractional and decimal form. Write fractional answers in lowest terms.

1. 0.9%   2. 0.17%

3. 0.25%   4. 0.39%

5. 0.5%   6. 0.32%

7. 0.52%   8. 0.45%

9. 0.58%   10. 0.65%

11. 0.8%   12. 0.76%

13. 0.83%   14. 0.7%

15. 0.62%   16. 0.75%

17. 0.15%   18. 0.71%

19. 0.6%   20. 0.95%

21. 0.72%   22. 0.94%

PRACTICE PERCENTS

Skill 3

WORKED EXAMPLE

$$\frac{1}{12}\% = \frac{1}{12} \times \frac{1}{100} = \frac{1}{1200}$$

$$\frac{1}{12}\% = \frac{1}{12} \times 0.01 \doteq 0.833 \times 0.01$$
$$= 0.00833$$

Write each percent in fractional and decimal form. Write fractional answers in lowest terms. Round decimal answers as needed.

1. $\frac{1}{5}\%$

2. $\frac{1}{4}\%$

3. $\frac{1}{10}\%$

4. $\frac{1}{2}\%$

5. $\frac{4}{5}\%$

6. $\frac{1}{20}\%$

7. $\frac{3}{10}\%$

8. $\frac{3}{4}\%$

9. $\frac{1}{25}\%$

10. $\frac{9}{20}\%$

11. $\frac{9}{10}\%$

12. $\frac{4}{25}\%$

13. $\frac{17}{20}\%$

14. $\frac{1}{3}\%$

15. $\frac{1}{6}\%$

16. $\frac{2}{9}\%$

17. $\frac{3}{8}\%$

18. $\frac{2}{3}\%$

19. $\frac{1}{16}\%$

20. $\frac{5}{12}\%$

ANSWERS

1. $\frac{1}{500}$; 0.002

2. $\frac{1}{400}$; 0.0025

3. $\frac{1}{1000}$; 0.001

4. $\frac{1}{200}$; 0.005

5. $\frac{1}{125}$; 0.008

6. $\frac{1}{2000}$; 0.0005

7. $\frac{3}{1000}$; 0.003

8. $\frac{3}{400}$; 0.0075

9. $\frac{1}{2500}$; 0.0004

10. $\frac{9}{2000}$; 0.0045

11. $\frac{9}{1000}$; 0.009

12. $\frac{1}{625}$; 0.0016

13. $\frac{17}{2000}$; 0.0085

14. $\frac{1}{300}$; 0.00333

15. $\frac{1}{600}$; 0.00167

16. $\frac{1}{450}$; 0.00222

17. $\frac{3}{800}$; 0.00375

18. $\frac{1}{150}$; 0.00667

19. $\frac{1}{1600}$; 0.000625

20. $\frac{1}{240}$; 0.00417

499

Complete the following chart. Write each percent in fractional and decimal form. Write fractional answers in lowest terms. Round decimal answers as needed.

ANSWERS

1. $\frac{1}{400}$; 0.0025
2. $\frac{1}{200}$; 0.005
3. $\frac{3}{10,000}$; 0.0003
4. $\frac{3}{400}$; 0.0075
5. $\frac{7}{1000}$; 0.007
6. $\frac{3}{500}$; 0.006
7. $\frac{3}{500}$; 0.006
8. $\frac{2}{625}$; 0.0032
9. $\frac{9}{2000}$; 0.0045
10. $\frac{1}{625}$; 0.0016
11. $\frac{39}{5000}$; 0.0078
12. $\frac{1}{150}$; 0.00667
13. $\frac{19}{2000}$; 0.0095
14. $\frac{1}{1200}$; 0.000833
15. $\frac{1}{120}$; 0.00833
16. $\frac{3}{800}$; 0.00375

		Fractional Form	Decimal Form
1.	$\frac{1}{4}$ %		
2.	$\frac{1}{2}$ %		
3.	0.03%		
4.	0.75%		
5.	$\frac{7}{10}$ %		
6.	$\frac{3}{5}$ %		
7.	0.6%		
8.	0.32%		
9.	$\frac{9}{20}$ %		
10.	$\frac{4}{25}$ %		
11.	0.78%		
12.	$\frac{2}{3}$ %		
13.	0.95%		
14.	$\frac{1}{12}$ %		
15.	$\frac{5}{6}$ %		
16.	$\frac{3}{8}$ %		

PERCENTS

OBJECTIVE   Skill 4   Rewrite mixed number and decimal
percents in fractional or decimal form.

SKILL MODEL

Write 102.5% in
fractional form.

PROBLEM

Write 102.5% in
decimal form.

$$102.5\% = 102\frac{1}{2}\% = \frac{205}{2}\% = \frac{205}{2} \times \frac{1}{100} = \frac{205}{200}$$

$$102.5\% = 102.5 \times 0.01 = 1.025$$

1

$$102.5\% = \frac{205}{200}$$
$$= 1\frac{1}{40}$$

$$102.5\% = 1.025$$

ANSWER

2

SOLUTION STEPS

Step 1   Percent means hundredths: multiply
102.5 by one hundredth.
To get a fractional answer, change
the decimal to an improper
fraction and multiply by one
hundredth in the form $\frac{1}{100}$.
To get a decimal answer, multiply
by one hundredth in the form 0.01

Step 2   Write the answers. Fractional
answers should be written in
lowest terms.

> **REMEMBER**
>
> To change FROM PERCENTS to fractions
> or decimals, always MULTIPLY BY ONE
> HUNDREDTH.

WORKED EXAMPLES

1. Write 2.2% as a fraction and
as a decimal.

$$2.2\% = 2\frac{2}{10}\% = \frac{22}{10} \times \frac{1}{100} = \frac{22}{1000}$$
$$= \frac{11}{500}$$

$$2.2\% = 2.2 \times 0.01 = 0.022$$

2. Write $3\frac{1}{3}\%$ as a fraction and
as a decimal.

$$3\frac{1}{3}\% = \frac{10}{3}\% = \frac{10}{3} \times \frac{1}{100} = \frac{1}{30}$$

$$3\frac{1}{3}\% \doteq 3.333 \doteq 3.333 \times 0.01$$
$$= 0.03333$$

BRUSH-UP EXERCISES

Write each percent in fractional and decimal form. Write fractional answers in lowest terms.

1. 7.4%

2. 6.25%

3. $113\frac{3}{4}\%$

4. $46\frac{2}{3}\%$

SELF-CHECK ANSWERS

1. $\frac{37}{500}$; 0.074   **2.** $\frac{1}{16}$; 0.0625   **3.** $1\frac{11}{80}$; 1.1375   **4.** $\frac{7}{15}$; $\doteq 0.46667$

ANSWERS

1. $\frac{3}{80}$; 0.0375

2. $\frac{9}{125}$; 0.072

3. $\frac{1}{8}$; 0.125

4. $\frac{29}{80}$; 0.3625

5. $\frac{13}{125}$; 0.104

6. $1\frac{1}{200}$; 1.005

7. $\frac{11}{250}$; 0.044

8. $\frac{17}{80}$; 0.2125

9. $\frac{101}{125}$; 0.808

10. $\frac{37}{40}$; 0.925

11. $1\frac{9}{80}$; 1.1125

12. $1\frac{1}{125}$; 1.008

13. $2\frac{11}{80}$; 2.1375

14. $2\frac{1}{250}$; 2.004

15. $3\frac{1}{8}$; 3.125

16. $3\frac{9}{80}$; 3.1125

WORKED EXAMPLE

$$237.5\% = 237\frac{1}{2}\% = \frac{475}{2}\% =$$

$$\frac{475}{2} \times \frac{1}{100} = \frac{475}{200} = 2\frac{75}{200} = 2\frac{3}{8}$$

$$237.5\% = 237.5 \times 0.01 = 2.375$$

Write each percent in fractional and decimal form. Write fractional answers in lowest terms.

1. 3.75%   2. 7.2%

3. 12.5%   4. 36.25%

5. 10.4%   6. 100.5%

7. 4.4%   8. 21.25%

9. 80.8%   10. 92.5%

11. 111.25%   12. 100.8%

13. 213.75%   14. 200.4%

15. 312.5%   16. 311.25%

WORKED EXAMPLE

$$110\frac{1}{4}\% = \frac{441}{4}\% = \frac{441}{4} \times \frac{1}{100}$$
$$= \frac{441}{400} = 1\frac{41}{100}$$

$$110\frac{1}{4}\% = 110.25\%$$
$$= 110.25 \times 0.01 = 1.1025$$

Write each percent in fractional and decimal form. Write fractional answers in lowest terms. Round decimal answers as needed.

1. $6\frac{1}{4}\%$

2. $22\frac{1}{2}\%$

3. $9\frac{3}{5}\%$

4. $18\frac{3}{4}\%$

5. $53\frac{1}{8}\%$

6. $63\frac{1}{5}\%$

7. $26\frac{2}{3}\%$

8. $79\frac{1}{6}\%$

9. $84\frac{4}{5}\%$

10. $91\frac{1}{9}\%$

11. $101\frac{1}{4}\%$

12. $237\frac{1}{2}\%$

13. $102\frac{1}{12}\%$

14. $211\frac{2}{3}\%$

15. $340\frac{4}{5}\%$

16. $303\frac{1}{8}\%$

1. $\frac{1}{16}$; 0.0625

2. $\frac{9}{40}$; 0.225

3. $\frac{12}{125}$; 0.096

4. $\frac{3}{16}$; 0.1875

5. $\frac{17}{32}$; 0.53125

6. $\frac{79}{125}$; 0.632

7. $\frac{4}{15}$; 0.26667

8. $\frac{19}{24}$; 0.79167

9. $\frac{106}{125}$; 0.848

10. $\frac{41}{45}$; 0.91111

11. $1\frac{1}{80}$; 1.0125

12. $2\frac{3}{8}$; 2.375

13. $1\frac{1}{48}$; 1.02083

14. $2\frac{7}{60}$; 2.11667

15. $3\frac{51}{125}$; 3.408

16. $3\frac{1}{32}$; 3.03125

Complete the following chart. Write each percent in fractional and decimal form. Write fractional answers in lowest terms. Round decimal answers as needed.

		Fractional Form	Decimal Form
1.	8.8%		
2.	18.75%		
3.	$5\frac{5}{8}$%		
4.	$31\frac{1}{4}$%		
5.	46.25%		
6.	50.4%		
7.	$43\frac{1}{3}$%		
8.	$74\frac{3}{8}$%		
9.	$93\frac{3}{4}$%		
10.	64.8%		
11.	86.25%		
12.	202.5%		
13.	$111\frac{1}{9}$%		
14.	$223\frac{1}{3}$%		
15.	$145\frac{5}{6}$%		
16.	303.75%		

Write each percent in fractional and decimal form. Write fractional answers in lowest terms. Round decimal answers as needed.

1. 7.5%

2. $3\frac{1}{8}$%

3. $17\frac{1}{2}$%

4. 24.4%

5. 51.25%

6. 62.5%

7. $89\frac{1}{3}$%

8. $95\frac{5}{6}$%

9. 108.75%

10. 120.8%

11. 231.25%

12. $154\frac{3}{8}$%

13. $222\frac{2}{9}$%

14. $304\frac{1}{6}$%

15. $214\frac{2}{3}$%

16. 412.5%

ANSWERS

1. $\frac{3}{40}$; 0.075

2. $\frac{1}{32}$; 0.03125

3. $\frac{7}{40}$; 0.175

4. $\frac{61}{250}$; 0.244

5. $\frac{41}{80}$; 0.5125

6. $\frac{5}{8}$; 0.625

7. $\frac{67}{75}$; 0.89333

8. $\frac{23}{24}$; 0.95833

9. $1\frac{7}{80}$; 1.0875

10. $1\frac{26}{125}$; 1.208

11. $2\frac{5}{16}$; 2.3125

12. $1\frac{87}{160}$; 1.54375

13. $2\frac{2}{9}$; 2.22222

14. $3\frac{1}{24}$; 3.04167

15. $2\frac{11}{75}$; 2.14667

16. $4\frac{1}{8}$; 4.125

SKILL 1

1. $\dfrac{11}{100}$; 0.11

2. 1; 1

3. $\dfrac{1}{4}$; 0.25

4. $\dfrac{18}{25}$; 0.72

SKILL 1 Write each percent in fractional and decimal form. Write fractional answers in lowest terms.

1. 11%

2. 100%

3. 25%

4. 72%

SKILL 2

1. $1\dfrac{23}{100}$; 1.23

2. 6; 6

3. $3\dfrac{3}{10}$; 3.3

4 $4\dfrac{7}{20}$; 4.35

SKILL 2 Write each percent in fractional and decimal form. Write fractional answers in lowest terms.

1. 123%

2. 600%

3. 330%

4. 435%

SKILL 3

1. $\dfrac{1}{1000}$; 0.001

2. $\dfrac{11}{2000}$; 0.0055

3. $\dfrac{3}{400}$; 0.0075

4. $\dfrac{1}{225}$; 0.00444

SKILL 3 Write each percent in fractional and decimal form. Write fractional answers in lowest terms. Round decimal answers as needed.

1. 0.1%

2. 0.55%

3. $\dfrac{3}{4}$%

4. $\dfrac{4}{9}$%

SKILL 4

1. $\dfrac{17}{40}$; 0.425

2. $1\dfrac{3}{125}$; 1.024

3. $\dfrac{39}{80}$; 0.4875

4. $2\dfrac{13}{24}$; 2.54167

SKILL 4 Write each percent in fractional and decimal form. Write fractional answers in lowest terms. Round decimal answers as needed.

1. 42.5%

2. 102.4%

3. $48\dfrac{3}{4}$%

4. $254\dfrac{1}{6}$%

OBJECTIVE   Skill 5   Rewrite decimals as percents.

SKILL MODEL

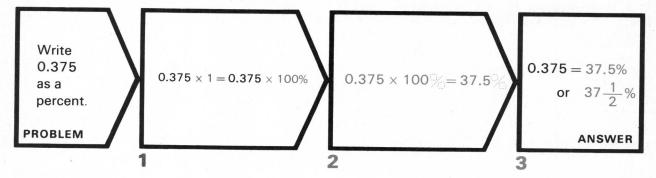

PROBLEM
Write 0.375 as a percent.

1
$0.375 \times 1 = 0.375 \times 100\%$

2
$0.375 \times 100\% = 37.5\%$

3
$0.375 = 37.5\%$
or $37\frac{1}{2}\%$

ANSWER

SOLUTION STEPS

Step 1   Write the product of the given decimal times 1, where 1 is in the form 100%.

Step 2   Multiply the given decimal by 100%.

Step 3   Write the answer as a percent. Fractional answers should be written in lowest terms.

> **REMEMBER**
> When you multiply a number by 1, the value of the number doesn't change.
> $$0.375 \times 1 = 0.375$$

> **UNDERSTAND**
> $$100\% = 100 \times \frac{1}{100} = \frac{100}{100} = 1$$
> or
> $$1 = 100\%$$

WORKED EXAMPLES

Write each decimal as a percent.

1. $0.06 = 0.06 \times 1$
$= 0.06 \times 100\%$
$= 6\%$

2. $0.544 = 0.544 \times 1$
$= 0.544 \times 100\%$
$= 54.4\%$
or $54\frac{2}{5}\%$

3. $2.007 = 2.007 \times 1$
$= 2.007 \times 100\%$
$= 200.7\%$
or $200\frac{7}{10}\%$

BRUSH-UP EXERCISES

Write each decimal as a percent. Write fractional answers in lowest terms.

1. 0.15

2. 0.01

3. 0.003

4. 0.105

5. 1.02

6. 3.012

SELF-CHECK ANSWERS

1. 15%   **2.** 1%   **3.** 0.3% or $\frac{3}{10}\%$ **4.** 10.5% or $10\frac{1}{2}\%$ **5.** 102%

6. 301.2% or $301\frac{1}{5}\%$

Write each decimal as a percent. Write fractional answers in lowest terms.

ANSWERS

1. 22%
2. 38%
3. 52%
4. 67%
5. 85%
6. 92%
7. 2%
8. 7%
9. 10%
10. 40%
11. 42.5% or $42\frac{1}{2}$%
12. 25.2% or $25\frac{1}{5}$%
13. 3.1% or $3\frac{1}{10}$%
14. 6.9% or $6\frac{9}{10}$%
15. 9.9% or $9\frac{9}{10}$%
16. 0.5% or $\frac{1}{2}$%
17. 0.2% or $\frac{1}{5}$%
18. 0.7% or $\frac{7}{10}$%

WORKED EXAMPLE

$$0.21 = 0.21 \times 1$$
$$= 0.21 \times 100\%$$
$$= 21\%$$

1. 0.22   2. 0.38
3. 0.52   4. 0.67
5. 0.85   6. 0.92
7. 0.02   8. 0.07
9. 0.1   10. 0.4
11. 0.425   12. 0.252
13. 0.031   14. 0.069
15. 0.099   16. 0.005
17. 0.002   18. 0.007

WORKED EXAMPLE
$3.47 = 3.47 \times 1$ $= 3.47 \times 100\%$ $= 347\%$

Write each decimal as a percent. Write fractional answers in lowest terms.

1. 3.21

2. 4.83

3. 1.57

4. 9.21

5. 6.08

6. 7.03

7. 4.05

8. 8.01

9. 3.1

10. 7.8

11. 5.123

12. 6.429

13. 7.011

14. 8.095

15. 5.082

16. 4.037

17. 8.006

18. 2.505

ANSWERS

1. 321%

2. 483%

3. 157%

4. 921%

5. 608%

6. 703%

7. 405%

8. 801%

9. 310%

10. 780%

11. 512.3% or $512\frac{3}{10}\%$

12. 642.9% or $642\frac{9}{10}\%$

13. 701.1% or $701\frac{1}{10}\%$

14. 809.5% or $809\frac{1}{2}\%$

15. 508.2% or $508\frac{1}{5}\%$

16. 403.7% or $403\frac{7}{10}\%$

17. 800.6% or $800\frac{3}{5}\%$

18. 250.5% or $250\frac{1}{2}\%$

Write each decimal as a percent. Write fractional answers in lowest terms.

1. 0.53   **2.** 0.69

3. 0.124   **4.** 0.3

5. 0.407   **6.** 0.002

7. 2.94   **8.** 5.23

9. 6.06   **10.** 8.07

11. 5.7   **12.** 4.9

13. 2.325   **14.** 4.459

15. 6.046   **16.** 8.025

17. 3.209   **18.** 5.102

19. 7.008   **20.** 9.003

510

OBJECTIVE   Skill 6   Rewrite fractions as percents.

SKILL MODEL

Write $\frac{1}{8}$ as a percent.

PROBLEM

$$\frac{1}{8} = 8\overline{)1.000}$$

$$\begin{array}{r} 0.125 \\ \hline -8 \\ \hline 20 \\ -16 \\ \hline 40 \\ -40 \\ \hline 0 \end{array}$$

1

$0.125 \times 100\% = 12.5\%$

2

$\frac{1}{8} = 12.5\%$

or $12\frac{1}{2}\%$

ANSWER

3

SOLUTION STEPS

Step 1   Write the given fraction as a decimal.

Step 2   Rewrite the decimal as a percent.

Step 3   Write the answer. Fractional answers should be written in lowest terms. Round decimal answers as needed.

WORKED EXAMPLES

Write each fraction as a percent.

1. $\frac{1}{4} = 4\overline{)1.00}$ with quotient 0.25

$0.25 \times 100\% = 25\%$

2. $\frac{2}{3} = 3\overline{)2.0000}$ with quotient $0.6666 = 0.66\frac{2}{3}$ $\doteq 0.667$

$0.66\frac{2}{3} \times 100\% = 66\frac{2}{3}\%$

or $0.667 \times 100\% = 66.7\%$

BRUSH-UP EXERCISES

Write each fraction as a percent. Fractional answers should be written in lowest terms. Round decimal answers as needed.

1. $\frac{1}{10}$ 2. $\frac{1}{2}$ 3. $\frac{3}{5}$

4. $\frac{3}{4}$ 5. $\frac{1}{16}$ 6. $\frac{2}{9}$

SELF-CHECK ANSWERS

1. 10%   2. 50%   3. 60%   4. 75%   5. $6\frac{1}{4}\%$ or 6.25%   6. $22\frac{2}{9}\% \doteq 22.2\%$

ANSWERS
1. 25%
2. 50%
3. 10%
4. 20%
5. 5%
6. 4%
7. 2%
8. 1%
9. 75%
10. 40%
11. 15%
12. 14%
13. 16%
14. 70%
15. 23%
16. 80%

WORKED EXAMPLE

$$\frac{3}{10} = 10\overline{)3.0} = 0.3$$

$$0.3 \times 100\% = 30\%$$

Write each fraction as a percent.

1. $\frac{1}{4}$

2. $\frac{1}{2}$

3. $\frac{1}{10}$

4. $\frac{1}{5}$

5. $\frac{1}{20}$

6. $\frac{1}{25}$

7. $\frac{1}{50}$

8. $\frac{1}{100}$

9. $\frac{3}{4}$

10. $\frac{2}{5}$

11. $\frac{3}{20}$

12. $\frac{7}{50}$

13. $\frac{4}{25}$

14. $\frac{7}{10}$

15. $\frac{23}{100}$

16. $\frac{4}{5}$

WORKED EXAMPLE

$$\frac{1}{3} = 3\overline{)1.0000}^{\,0.3333\,\doteq\,0.333}$$

$$\frac{1}{3} = 0.33\frac{1}{3} \times 100\% = 33\frac{1}{3}\%$$

$$\frac{1}{3} \doteq 0.333 \times 0.01\% = 33.3\%$$

Write each fraction as a percent. Write fractional answers in lowest terms. Round decimal answers as needed.

1. $\dfrac{1}{8}$

2. $\dfrac{1}{12}$

3. $\dfrac{1}{16}$

4. $\dfrac{1}{9}$

5. $\dfrac{1}{6}$

6. $\dfrac{2}{3}$

7. $\dfrac{3}{8}$

8. $\dfrac{5}{16}$

9. $\dfrac{7}{12}$

10. $\dfrac{4}{9}$

11. $\dfrac{5}{6}$

12. $\dfrac{11}{16}$

ANSWERS

1. $12\frac{1}{2}\%$ or 12.5%

2. $8\frac{1}{3}\%$ $\doteq$ 8.3%

3. $6\frac{1}{4}\%$ or 6.25%

4. $11\frac{1}{9}\%$ $\doteq$ 11.1%

5. $16\frac{2}{3}\%$ $\doteq$ 16.7%

6. $66\frac{2}{3}\%$ $\doteq$ 66.7%

7. $37\frac{1}{2}\%$ or 37.5%

8. $31\frac{1}{4}\%$ or 31.25%

9. $58\frac{1}{3}\%$ $\doteq$ 58.3%

10. $44\frac{4}{9}\%$ $\doteq$ 44.4%

11. $83\frac{1}{3}\%$ $\doteq$ 83.3%

12. $68\frac{3}{4}\%$ or 68.75%

Write each fraction as a percent. Write fractional answers in lowest terms. Round decimal answers as needed.

ANSWERS
1. 75%
2. 20%
3. 30%
4. $33\frac{1}{3}$% $\doteq$ 33.3%
5. $16\frac{2}{3}$% $\doteq$ 16.7%
6. 35%
7. 16%
8. $22\frac{2}{9}$% $\doteq$ 22.2%
9. $83\frac{1}{3}$% $\doteq$ 83.3%
10. $66\frac{2}{3}$% $\doteq$ 66.7%
11. $37\frac{1}{2}$% or 37.5%
12. $44\frac{4}{9}$% $\doteq$ 44.4%
13. $41\frac{2}{3}$% $\doteq$ 41.7%
14. $43\frac{3}{4}$% or 40.75%

1. $\dfrac{3}{4}$

2. $\dfrac{1}{5}$

3. $\dfrac{3}{10}$

4. $\dfrac{1}{3}$

5. $\dfrac{1}{6}$

6. $\dfrac{7}{20}$

7. $\dfrac{4}{25}$

8. $\dfrac{2}{9}$

9. $\dfrac{5}{6}$

10. $\dfrac{2}{3}$

11. $\dfrac{3}{8}$

12. $\dfrac{4}{9}$

13. $\dfrac{5}{12}$

14. $\dfrac{7}{16}$

OBJECTIVE   Skill 7   Rewrite whole numbers and mixed numbers as percents.

SKILL MODEL

PROBLEM	1&2	3	ANSWER
Write $3\frac{1}{16}$ as a percent.	$3\frac{1}{16} = \frac{49}{16}$ $\frac{49}{16} = 16\overline{)49.0000}\,^{3.0625}$	$3.0625 \times 100\% = 306.25\%$	$3\frac{1}{16} = 306.25\%$ or $306\frac{1}{4}\%$

SOLUTION STEPS

Step 1   Write the given mixed number as an improper fraction.

Step 2   Rewrite the improper fraction as a decimal.

Step 3   Rewrite the decimal as a percent.

Step 4   Write the answer. Fractional answers should be written in lowest terms.

WORKED EXAMPLES

Write each number as a percent.

1. $4 = 4 \times 100\% = 400\%$

2. $2\frac{1}{4} = \frac{9}{4} = 4\overline{)9.00}\,^{2.25}$
   $2.25 \times 100\% = 225\%$

3. $2\frac{2}{3} = \frac{8}{3} = 3\overline{)8.0000}\,^{2.6666} \doteq 2.667$ or $2.66\frac{2}{3}$
   $2.667 \times 100\% = 266.7\%$
   or $2.66\frac{2}{3} \times 100\% = 266\frac{2}{3}\%$

BRUSH-UP EXERCISES

Write each number as a percent.

1. 1   2. 3   3. $2\frac{1}{2}$

4. $7\frac{3}{10}$ 5. $4\frac{3}{8}$ 6. $1\frac{1}{6}$

SELF-CHECK ANSWERS

1. 100%   2. 300%   3. 250%   4. 730%   5. 437.5% or $437\frac{1}{2}\%$ 6. $116\frac{2}{3}\% \doteq 116.7\%$

WORKED EXAMPLE

$$1\frac{1}{5} = \frac{6}{5}$$

$$\frac{6}{5} = 5\overline{)6.0}^{1.2}$$

$$1.2 = 1.2 \times 100\% = 120\%$$

Write each number as a percent. Write fractional answers in lowest terms. Round decimal answers as needed.

1. $3\frac{1}{2}$

2. $2\frac{1}{10}$

3. $1\frac{1}{4}$

4. $6\frac{4}{5}$

5. $3\frac{3}{10}$

6. $2\frac{1}{20}$

7. $1\frac{23}{100}$

8. 5

9. $2\frac{7}{50}$

10. $6\frac{1}{8}$

11. $7\frac{1}{3}$

12. $4\frac{1}{16}$

516

PERCENTS

```
WORKED EXAMPLE
          4 2/3 = 14/3

        4.6666 = 4.66 2/3 ≐ 4.667
   3 ) 14.0000
   4.66 2/3 × 100% = 466 2/3 %
   4.667 × 100% = 466.7%
```

Write each number as a percent. Write
fractional answers in lowest terms.
Round decimal answers as needed.

1. $3\frac{3}{4}$

2. $1\frac{4}{25}$

3. $2\frac{7}{10}$

4. $6\frac{3}{5}$

5. $4\frac{1}{9}$

6. $5\frac{13}{20}$

7. $3\frac{3}{16}$

8. 2

9. $1\frac{5}{8}$

10. $4\frac{4}{9}$

11. $2\frac{5}{12}$

12. $3\frac{3}{8}$

SKILL 5

1. 4%

2. $59\frac{3}{5}$% or 59.6%

3. $\frac{17}{50}$% or 0.34%

4. $206\frac{9}{10}$% or 206.9%

SKILL 6

1. 50%

2. 5%

3. $37\frac{1}{2}$% or 37.5%

4. $22\frac{2}{9}$% $\doteq$ 22.2%

SKILL 7

1. 310%

2. 600%

3. $137\frac{1}{2}$% or 137.5%

4. $244\frac{4}{9}$% $\doteq$ 244.4%

SKILL 5 Write each decimal as a percent. Write fractional answers in lowest terms.

1. 0.04   **2.** 0.596

3. 0.0034   **4.** 2.069

SKILL 6 Write each fraction as a percent. Write fractional answers in lowest terms. Round decimal answers as needed.

1. $\frac{1}{2}$ **2.** $\frac{1}{20}$

3. $\frac{3}{8}$ **4.** $\frac{2}{9}$

SKILL 7 Write each number as a percent. Write fractional answers in lowest terms. Round decimal answers as needed.

1. $3\frac{1}{10}$ **2.** 6

3. $1\frac{3}{8}$ **4.** $2\frac{4}{9}$

LESSON　　　　　　　PERCENTS　　　　　Skill 8

OBJECTIVE　　　　Skill 8　　Find a percentage of a given number.

SKILL MODEL

PROBLEM

2.5%
of 80
is what
number?

1

2.5%　of 80　is　what number?
↓　　↓　　↓　　↓　　↓
0.025　×　80　=　n
percent × base = percentage

2

$0.025 \times 80 = n$
$2.000 = n$
or
$n = 2$

3

2.5%
of 80
is 2

ANSWER

SOLUTION STEPS

Step 1　Write an equation. Use n to hold the place of the unknown number. Change the percent to a decimal. [See Percents Lesson 4.]

Step 2　Solve the equation by multiplying.

Step 3　Write the answer.

NOTE

The product of a percent (rate) times a base number is the percentage.

$5\% \times 150 = 7.5$
percent × base = percentage

PROPORTION METHOD

[See Proportions Lessons 5 & 6.]

$\frac{2.5}{100}$ ✕ $\frac{p}{80}$ ⟹ $\frac{100 \times p}{2.5 \times 80}$

$2.5 \times 80 = 100 \times p$
$2 = p$

WORKED EXAMPLES

1. 7% of 180 is what number?
   (7% = 0.07)
   $0.07 \times 180 = n$
   $12.6 = n$
   7% of 180 is 12.6

2. What is 265% of $12?
   (265% = 2.65)
   $2.65 \times \$12 = n$
   $\$31.80 = n$
   $31.80 is 265% of $12

3. Find $12\frac{1}{2}$% of 240.
   ($12\frac{1}{2}$% = 0.125)
   $0.125 \times 240 = n$
   $30 = n$
   $12\frac{1}{2}$% of 240 is 30

BRUSH-UP EXERCISES

1. 6% of 90 is what number?

2. 85% of 60 is what number?

3. What is 150% of $400?

4. What is 0.5% of 62?

5. 7.5% of 250 = ?

6. $6\frac{1}{4}$% of $320 = ?

SELF-CHECK ANSWERS

1. 5.4　　2. 51　　3. $600　　4. 0.31　　5. 18.75　　6. $20

ANSWERS
1. 3.2
2. 30¢
3. 1.2
4. 0.92
5. 5.76
6. 32
7. 31.5
8. $14
9. 8
10. 8.4
11. 1.32
12. 0.246
13. 1.98

WORKED EXAMPLE

9% of 40 is what number?
↓   ↓ ↓ ↓ ↓
0.09   ×   40 $= n$

3.6 $= n$

Solve.

1. 8% of 40 is what number?

2. 3% of $10 is what amount?

3. 4% of 30 is what number?

4. 2% of 46 is what number?

5. 9% of 64 is what number?

6. 8% of 400 is what number?

7. 9% of 350 is what number?

8. 7% of $200 is what amount?

9. 8% of 100 is what number?

10. 5% of 168 is what number?

11. 6% of 22 is what number?

12. 1% of 24.6 is what number?

13. 5% of 39.6 is what number?

PRACTICE

PERCENTS

Skill 8

page 2

WORKED EXAMPLE

What is 56% of 72?

56% of 72 is what number?

↓   ↓ ↓ ↓ ↓

$0.56 \times 72 = n$

$40.32 = n$

Solve.

1. What is 14% of 20?

2. What is 16% of 80?

3. What is 15% of $60?

4. What is 36% of 20?

5. What is 54% of 21?

6. What is 72% of 54?

7. What is 65% of 30?

8. What is 18% of 36?

9. What is 11% of 44?

10. What is 50% of 500?

11. What is 30% of 175?

12. What is 60% of $52.60?

13. What is 45% of 615.2?

ANSWERS

1. 2.8

2. 12.8

3. $9

4. 7.2

5. 11.34

6. 38.88

7. 19.5

8. 6.48

9. 4.84

10. 250

11. 52.5

12. $31.56

13. 276.84

521

ANSWERS
1. 75
2. $54
3. 96
4. 140
5. 43.5
6. 56
7. 150
8. 45
9. 198
10. $97.90
11. 1890
12. 368.13
13. 99.47

WORKED EXAMPLE

125% of 30 = ?
↓ ↓ ↓ ↓ ↓
1.25 × 30 = n
37.5 = n

Solve.

1. 250% of 30 = ?

2. 120% of $45 = ?

3. 240% of 40 = ?

4. 175% of 80 = ?

5. 290% of 15 = ?

6. 280% of 20 = ?

7. 300% of 50 = ?

8. 125% of 36 = ?

9. 275% of 72 = ?

10. 110% of $89 = ?

11. 315% of 600 = ?

12. 105% of 350.6 = ?

13. 145% of 68.6 = ?

WORKED EXAMPLE

Find 0.25% of 80.

0.25% of 72 is what number?

$$\downarrow \quad \downarrow \quad \downarrow \quad \downarrow \quad \downarrow$$

$$0.0025 \times 80 = n$$

$$0.2 = n$$

Solve.

1. Find 0.7% of 90.

2. Find 0.6% of 60.

3. Find 0.9% of 80.

4. Find 3.7% of 90.

5. Find 2.5% of $110.

6. Find 8.5% of 70.

7. Find 7.3% of 2000.

8. Find $\frac{1}{4}$% of $160.

9. Find $\frac{1}{8}$% of 200.

10. Find $8\frac{1}{4}$% of 90.

11. Find $8\frac{3}{4}$% of 1000.

12. Find $7\frac{1}{2}$% of 150.8

13. Find $6\frac{1}{5}$% of 55.5

ANSWERS

1. 0.63
2. 0.36
3. 0.72
4. 3.33
5. $2.75
6. 5.95
7. 146
8. 40¢
9. 0.25
10. 7.425
11. 87.5
12. 11.31
13. 3.441

523

ANSWERS

1. 9.72

2. $378

3. $14.25

4. 4.5

5. 77.28

6. 3.432

7. $16.10

8. 1.971

9. 360

10. $7

11. 289.75

12. 7.806

13. 404.04

WORKED EXAMPLE

$$66\frac{2}{3}\% \text{ of } 921 = ?$$
$$\downarrow \qquad \downarrow \quad \downarrow \quad \downarrow \quad \downarrow$$
$$\frac{2}{3} \qquad \times \quad 921 = n$$
$$614 = n$$

$$\left(\text{We use the fact that } 66\frac{2}{3}\% = \frac{2}{3}.\right)$$

Solve.

1. What number is 18% of 54?

2. What is 105% of $360?

3. 15% of $95 = ?

4. Find $\frac{1}{2}$% of 900.

5. What number is $9\frac{1}{5}$% of 840?

6. 6.6% of 52 = ?

7. What is $5\frac{3}{4}$% of $280?

8. Find 0.3% of 657.

9. What number is 225% of 160?

10. What is 0.7% of $1000?

11. $30\frac{1}{2}$% of 950 = ?

12. What is 1.2% of 650.5?

13. Find $33\frac{1}{3}$% of 1212.12

OBJECTIVE   Skill 9   Find what percent one
number is of another number.

SKILL MODEL

What %
of 80
is 44?

PROBLEM

What % of 80 is 44?
$\downarrow$ $\downarrow$ $\downarrow$ $\downarrow$ $\downarrow$
n $\times$ 80 $=$ 44
percent $\times$ base $=$ percentage

1

$n \times 80 = 44$

$\dfrac{n \times \overset{1}{\cancel{80}}}{\underset{1}{\cancel{80}}} = \dfrac{44}{80}$

$n = 0.55$
$n = 55\%$

2

55%
of 80
is 44

ANSWER

3

SOLUTION STEPS

Step 1   Write an equation. Use n to hold
the place of the unknown percent.

Step 2   Solve the equation for n by
dividing both sides by 80.

Step 3   Write the answer.

PROPORTION METHOD
[See Proportions Lessons 5 & 6.]

$\dfrac{p}{100} \bowtie \dfrac{44}{80} \Rightarrow \dfrac{100 \times 44}{p \times 80}$

$80 \times p = 100 \times 44$
$p = 55$
$\dfrac{p}{100} = 55\%$

WORKED EXAMPLES

1. What % of 56 is 14?

$n \times 56 = 14$

$n = \dfrac{14}{56}$

$\begin{array}{r} 0.25 \\ 56\overline{)14.00} \end{array}$

$n = 0.25$

$n = 25\%$

2. 250 is what % of 125?

$n \times 125 = 250$

$n = \dfrac{250}{125}$

$\begin{array}{r} 2 \\ 125\overline{)250} \end{array}$

$n = 2$

$n = 200\%$

3. What % of 80 is 6?

$n \times 80 = 6$

$n = \dfrac{6}{80}$

$\begin{array}{r} 0.075 \\ 80\overline{)6.000} \end{array}$

$n = 0.075$

$n = 7.5\%$ or $7\frac{1}{2}\%$

BRUSH-UP EXERCISES

1. What % of 60 is 3?

2. What % of 90 is 54?

3. $16 is what % of $80?

4. 84 is what % of 21?

5. What % of 6400 is 8?

6. What % of 48 is 42?

SELF-CHECK ANSWERS

1. 5%   **2.** 60%   **3.** 20%   **4.** 400%   **5.** 0.125%   **6.** 87.5% or $87\frac{1}{2}\%$

ANSWERS
1. 5%
2. 3%
3. 10%
4. 5%
5. 4%
6. 8%
7. 1%
8. 25%
9. 20%
10. 5%
11. 5%
12. 9%
13. 7%

WORKED EXAMPLE

What % of 20 is 2

$n \times 20 = 2$

$n = \dfrac{2}{20}$

$n = 0.10 = 10\%$

Solve.

1. What % of 120 is 6?

2. What % of 100 is 3?

3. What % of 50 is 5?

4. What % of 360 is 18?

5. What % of 150 is 6?

6. What % of 75 is 6?

7. What % of 1000 is 10?

8. What % of $1.00 is 25¢?

9. What % of 920 is 184?

10. What % of $100 is $5?

11. What % of 760 is 38?

12. What % of 340 is $30.60?

13. What % of 1250 is 87.5?

PRACTICE

PERCENTS

Skill 9

page 2

```
WORKED EXAMPLE
What  %  of  $80  is  $41.60
  ↓    ↓   ↓    ↓    ↓
  n    ×   $80 = $41.60
              n = $41.60
                  ──────
                    $80
              n = 0.52 = 52%
```

Solve.

1. What % of 72 is 18?

2. What % of 100 is 45?

3. What % of 125 is 25?

4. What % of 600 is 210?

5. What % of 45 is 8.1?

6. What % of $90 is $25.20?

7. What % of 225 is 108?

8. What % of 24 is 14.4?

9. What % of 250 is 90?

10. What % of $85 is $52.70?

11. What % of 160 is 115.2?

12. What % of 180 is 115.2?

13. What % of 1260 is 466.2?

ANSWERS

1. 25%
2. 45%
3. 20%
4. 35%
5. 18%
6. 28%
7. 48%
8. 60%
9. 36%
10. 62%
11. 72%
12. 64%
13. 37%

527

ANSWERS	
1.	200%
2.	150%
3.	125%
4.	115%
5.	250%
6.	600%
7.	106%
8.	107%
9.	180%
10.	175%
11.	140%
12.	250%
13.	113%

WORKED EXAMPLE

81 is what % of 60?

What % of 60 is 81?

$$n \times 60 = 81$$
$$n = \frac{81}{60}$$
$$n = 1.35 = 135\%$$

Solve.

1. 20 is what % of 10?

2. 93 is what % of 62?

3. 175 is what % of 140?

4. $414 is what % of $360?

5. 60 is what % of 24?

6. 90 is what % of 15?

7. $159 is what % of $150?

8. 85.6 is what % of 80?

9. 324 is what % of 180?

10. 108.5 is what % of 62?

11. $966 is what % of $690?

12. 237.5 is what % of 95?

13. $2172.99 is what % of $1923?

WORKED EXAMPLE

What % of 700 is 246.4?

$n \times 700 = 246.4$

$n = \dfrac{246.4}{700}$

$n = 0.352 = 35.2\%$

or $35\dfrac{1}{5}\%$

Solve.

1. What % of 400 is 10?

2. What % of 800 is 100?

3. What % of 1260 is 6.3?

4. What % of 1500 is 19.5?

5. What % of 390 is 260?

6. What % of 740 is 77.7?

7. What % of $750 is $99.75?

8. What % of $2000 is $155?

9. What % of 416 is 219.44?

10. What % of $900 is $30?

11. What % of 950 is 172.9?

12. What % of 30 is 12.21?

13. What % of 560 is 590.8?

ANSWERS

1. 2.5%
2. 12.5%
3. 0.5%
4. 1.3%
5. $66\dfrac{2}{3}\%$ $\doteq 66.7\%$
6. 10.5%
7. 13.3%
8. 7.75%
9. 52.75%
10. $3\dfrac{1}{3}\%$ $\doteq 3.3\%$
11. 18.2%
12. 40.7%
13. 105.5%

529

ANSWERS

1. 50%

2. 3%

3. 3%

4. 32.5%

5. 45%

6. 18%

7. 56%

8. $166\frac{2}{3}\%$
   $\doteq 166.7\%$

9. 6.75%

10. 111%

11. 250%

12. $133\frac{1}{3}\%$
   $\doteq 133.3\%$

13. 112.5%

WORKED EXAMPLE

What % of 129 is 215?

$\downarrow \quad \downarrow \quad \downarrow \quad \downarrow \quad \downarrow$

$n \quad \times \; 129 = 215$

$$n = \frac{215}{129}$$

$$n = 166\frac{2}{3}\% \doteq 166.7\%$$

Solve.

1. What % of 32 is 16?

2. What % of 70 is 2.1?

3. What % of $120 is $3.60?

4. 195 is what % of 600?

5. What % of $90 is $40.50?

6. What % of 215 is 38.7?

7. 476 is what % of 850?

8. What % of 3 is 5?

9. What % of $160 is $10.80?

10. What % of 1800 is 1998?

11. $39 is what % of $15.60?

12. What % of 90 is 120?

13. What % of $220 is $247.50?

OBJECTIVE　　　Skill 10　Find a number if a percentage of the number is known.

SKILL MODEL

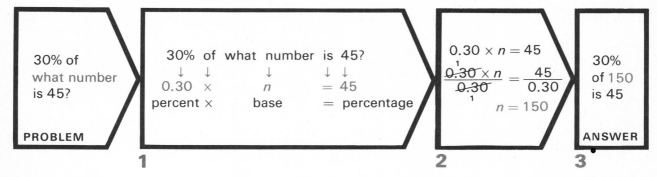

SOLUTION STEPS

Step 1　Write an equation using n to hold the place of the unknown number. Change the % to a decimal. [See Percents Lesson 4.]

Step 2　Solve the equation for n by dividing both sides by 0.30 [See Decimals Lesson 12.]

Step 3　Write the answer.

PROPORTION METHOD
[See Proportions Lessons 5 & 6.]

$$\frac{30}{100} \diagup\!\!\!\!\diagdown \frac{45}{p} \Rightarrow \begin{array}{c} 100 \times 45 \\ 30 \times p \end{array}$$

$$30 \times p = 100 \times 45$$
$$p = 150$$

WORKED EXAMPLES

1. 8% of what number is 6?

$0.08 \times n = 6$

$n = \dfrac{6}{0.08} = 75$

8% of 75 is 6

2. 81 is 225% of what number?

$2.25 \times n = 81$

$n = \dfrac{81}{2.25} = 36$

225% of 36 is 81

3. 2.5% of what number is 10?

$0.025 \times n = 10$

$n = \dfrac{10}{0.025} = 400$

2.5% of 400 is 10

BRUSH-UP EXERCISES

1. 6% of what number is 3?

2. 30% of what number is 75?

3. $150 is 75% of what amount?

4. 185% of what number is 148?

5. 4 is $\dfrac{1}{4}$% of what number?

6. $62\dfrac{1}{2}$% of what number is 40?

SELF-CHECK ANSWERS

1. 50　　**2.** 250　　**3.** $200　　**4.** 80　　**5.** 1600　　**6.** 64

531

ANSWERS

1. 80
2. $62.50
3. 22
4. $200
5. $80
6. 200
7. 30
8. 65
9. 48
10. 112.5
11. 12
12. 160
13. 144

WORKED EXAMPLE

5% of what number is 3?

$$0.05 \times n = 3$$
$$n = \frac{3}{0.05}$$
$$n = 60$$

5% of 60 is 3

Solve.

1. 5% of what number is 4?

2. 8% of what amount is $5?

3. 10% of what number is 2.2?

4. 9% of what amount is $18?

5. 20% of what amount is $16?

6. 7% of what number is 14?

7. 35% of what number is 10.5?

8. 60% of what number is 39?

9. 96% of what number is 46.08?

10. 16% of what number is 18?

11. 63% of what number is 7.56?

12. 15% of what number is 24?

13. 44% of what number is 63.36?

WORKED EXAMPLE

250 is 200% of what number?

$\underset{\downarrow}{200\%} \underset{\downarrow}{\text{of}} \underset{\downarrow}{\text{what number}} \underset{\downarrow}{\text{is}} \underset{\downarrow}{250?}$

$$2 \times n = 250$$

$$n = \frac{250}{2} = 125$$

250 is 200% of 125

Solve.

1. 100% of what number is 78?

2. 150% of what number is 96?

3. 250% of what number is 75?

4. 160% of what number is 352?

5. 400 is 400% of what number?

6. 63.7 is 175% of what number?

7. 793 is 325% of what number?

8. $504 is 120% of what amount?

9. $100 is 1000% of what amount?

10. 500% of what number is 50.5?

11. 276% of what number is 138?

12. 265% of what number is 609.5?

13. 134% of what number is 89.78?

ANSWERS

1. 78

2. 64

3. 30

4. 220

5. 100

6. 36.4

7. 244

8. $420

9. $10

10. 10.1

11. 50

12. 230

13. 67

ANSWERS
1. 1200
2. 65,600
3. $300,000
4. $2000
5. $2400
6. 550
7. 12,000
8. 864
9. 1000
10. 1375
11. 1664
12. 848
13. 3.5

WORKED EXAMPLE

$\frac{1}{2}$ % of what amount is $3?

$0.005 \times n = \$3$

$n = \dfrac{\$3}{0.005}$

$n = \$600$

Solve.

1. 0.25% of what number is 3?

2. $\frac{1}{8}$% of what number is 82?

3. 0.1% of what amount is $300?

4. $\frac{2}{5}$% of what amount is $8?

5. $\frac{7}{8}$% of what amount is $21?

6. 1.1 is 0.2% of what number?

7. 72 is 0.6% of what number?

8. 3.24 is $\frac{3}{8}$% of what number?

9. 7.5 is $\frac{3}{4}$% of what number?

10. 2.75 is 0.2% of what number?

11. 0.25% of what number is 4.16?

12. $\frac{5}{8}$% of what number is 5.3?

13. 0.7% of what number is 0.0245?

WORKED EXAMPLE

37.5% of what number is 12?

$\downarrow$ $\downarrow$ $\downarrow$ $\downarrow$ $\downarrow$

$0.375 \times \quad\quad n \quad = 12$

$$n = \frac{12}{0.375}$$

$$n = 32$$

Solve.

1. 6.25% of what number is 16?

2. 1.5% of what number is 15?

3. $15\frac{1}{2}$% of what amount is $341?

4. $12\frac{1}{2}$% of what amount is $122.25?   **5.** $8\frac{3}{4}$% of what amount is $42?

6. 5.64% of what number is 35.25?   **7.** 26.6% of what number is 11.97?

8. 61.05 is 55.5% of what number?   **9.** 13.52 is $12\frac{1}{2}$% of what number?

10. 7.25% of what amount is $108.75?   **11.** 10% of what amount is $10.95?

12. 225.25% of what number is 135.15?   **13.** $100\frac{1}{2}$% of what number is 402?

ANSWERS

1. 256

2. 1000

3. $2200

4. $978

5. $480

6. 625

7. 45

8. 110

9. 108.16

10. $1500

11. $109.50

12. 60

13. 400

535

SKILL 8

1. 8

2. 8.1

3. 437.5

4. $31.50

SKILL 8

1. 4% of 200 is what number?

2. What number is 18% of 45?

3. 175% of 250 is what number?

4. Find $5\frac{1}{4}$% of $600.

SKILL 9

1. 35%

2. 26%

3. 115%

4. $66\frac{2}{3}$% $\doteq$ 66.7%

SKILL 9

1. What % of 180 is 63?

2. What % of 95 is 24.7?

3. $184 is what % of $160?

4. What % of 78 is 52?

SKILL 10

1. 75

2. 25

3. 220

4. $6800

SKILL 10

1. 12% of what number is 9?

2. 29 is 116% of what number?

3. 138% of what number is 303.6?

4. $6\frac{1}{4}$% of what amount is $425?

PERCENTS
Unit Mastery Test – Page 1
Answers on Page 542

SKILL 1   Write each percent in fractional and decimal form. Write fractional answers in lowest terms.

1. 9%   **2.** 70%   **3.** 84%

SKILL 2   Write each percent in fractional and decimal form. Write fractional answers in lowest terms.

1. 313%   **2.** 400%   **3.** 665%

SKILL 3   Write each percent in fractional and decimal form. Write fractional answers in lowest terms.

1. 0.45%   **2.** $\frac{1}{5}$%   **3.** $\frac{5}{12}$%

SKILL 4   Write each percent in fractional and decimal form. Write fractional answers in lowest terms. Round decimal answers as needed.

1. 53.75%   **2.** $23\frac{1}{3}$%   **3.** $121\frac{3}{5}$%

SKILL 5   Write each decimal as a percent. Write fractions in lowest terms.

1. 0.07   **2.** 0.685   **3.** 4.013

SKILL 1

1.

2.

3.

SKILL 2

1.

2.

3.

SKILL 3

1.

2.

3.

SKILL 4

1.

2.

3.

SKILL 5

1.

2.

3.

Unit Mastery Test – Page 2

Answers on Page 542

SKILL 6

1.

2.

3.

SKILL 6   Write each fraction as a mixed number percent or decimal percent. Write fractions in lowest terms. Round decimal answers as needed.

1. $\dfrac{1}{5}$

2. $\dfrac{5}{8}$

3. $\dfrac{5}{6}$

SKILL 7

1.

2.

3.

SKILL 7   Write each number as a mixed number percent or decimal percent. Write fractions in lowest terms. Round decimal answers as needed.

1. $2\dfrac{1}{5}$

2. $2\dfrac{1}{6}$

3. $2\dfrac{2}{3}$

SKILL 8

1.

2.

3.

SKILL 8

1. 16% of 180 is what number?

2. What is 215% of $72?

3. Find $10\dfrac{3}{4}$% of 2400.

SKILL 9

1.

2.

3.

SKILL 9

1. What % of 60 is 27?

2. $161 is what % of $140?

3. What % of 60 is 7.5?

SKILL 10

1.

2.

3.

SKILL 10

1. 32% of what number is 24?

2. $96 is 160% of what amount?

3. 16.5% of what number is 13.2?

DECIMALS, PROPORTIONS, AND PERCENTS

Module Mastery Test – Page 1

Answers on Page 541

UNIT 10   DECIMALS

SKILL 1 Write as a decimal.

215 and 233 ten-thousandths

SKILL 2 Round to the nearest tenth.

18.55

SKILL 3 Write as a decimal.

$6\frac{3}{10}$

SKILL 4 Write as a mixed number in lowest terms.

19.65

SKILL 5

```
   2.18
+ 35.704
```

SKILL 6

```
   9.873
+ 10.349
```

SKILL 7

```
  86.738
-  5.52
```

SKILL 8

```
  596.8025
-  39.924
```

SKILL 9

```
  5.89
× 76
```

SKILL 10

```
  46.82
× 7.05
```

SKILL 11

18)528.3

SKILL 12

82.8)62.1

UNIT 11   PROPORTIONS

SKILL 1 Write the ratio as a fraction in simplest form.

84 lb to 20 lb

SKILL 2 Write the rate in simplest form, using a fraction.

96 km on 9L

SKILL 3 Find the unit rate. Round to the nearest tenth.

92 km in 8 min

UNIT 11

4.

5.

6.

UNIT 11   PROPORTIONS

SKILL 4 Tell if the proportion is TRUE or NOT TRUE.

$$\frac{14}{15} \stackrel{?}{=} \frac{24}{25}$$

SKILL 5 Find the unknown value. Check the answer.

$$\frac{16}{d} = \frac{112}{77}$$

SKILL 6 Write and solve the proportion.

168 ft in 7 sec = x ft in 8 sec

UNIT 12

1.

2.

3.

4.

5.

6.

7.

8.

9.

10.

UNIT 12   PERCENTS

SKILL 1 Write in fractional and decimal form.

48%

SKILL 2 Write in fractional and decimal form.

425%

SKILL 3 Write in fractional and decimal form.

$$\frac{2}{5}\%$$

SKILL 4 Write in fractional and decimal form.

$$81\frac{1}{4}\%$$

SKILL 5 Write as a percent.

0.542

SKILL 6 Write as a percent.

$$\frac{5}{16}$$

SKILL 7 Write as a percent.

$$7\frac{3}{4}$$

SKILL 8 What is 215% of 85?

SKILL 9 What percent of 115 is 13.8?

SKILL 10   84 is 140% of what number?

Module C Test

Unit 10 Skills 1–12

1. 10.018   2. 6.08   3. 9.07   4. $24\frac{3}{20}$ 5. 75.984   6. 20.33   7. 26.225

8. 123.985   9. 475.2   10. 252.7174   11. 1.28   12. 1.35

Unit 11 Skills 1–6

1. $\frac{48}{5}$ 2. $\frac{\$45}{4\ hr}$ 3. 9.7 mi per min   4. TRUE   5. 18   6. 525 (km)

Unit 12 Skills 1–10

1. $\frac{11}{20}$; 0.55   2. $3\frac{1}{2}$; 3.5   3. $\frac{3}{2000}$; 0.0015   4. $\frac{91}{125}$; 0.728   5. $73\frac{1}{2}$% or 73.5%

6. $87\frac{1}{2}$% or 87.5%   7. 340%   8. 112.1   9. 18%   10. 45

Unit 10 Test

Skill 1   1. 6.3974   2. 2123.075   3. 601.09

Skill 2   1. 6.85   2. 4.9   3. 8.720

Skill 3   1. 6.03   2. 0.65   3. 5.111

Skill 4   1. $\frac{1}{20}$ 2. $9\frac{6}{25}$ 3. $8\frac{27}{1000}$

Skill 5   1. $28.97   2. 28.647   3. 19.677

Skill 6   1. $111.08   2. 218.53   3. 764.203

Skill 7   1. $112.13   2. 146.146   3. 62.22

Skill 8   1. $58.89   2. 179.7929   3. 2.871

Skill 9   1. 28.42   2. 1166.59   3. 13563.165

Skill 10   1. 5.224   2. 55.0544   3. 27.4845

Skill 11   1. 4.8   2. 0.32   3. 0.025

Skill 12   1. 7.1   2. 7.22   3. 2.05

Unit 11 Test

Skill 1   1. $\frac{7}{2}$ 2. $\frac{8}{3}$ 3. $\frac{5}{3}$

Skill 2   1. $\frac{15\ km}{2\ L}$ 2. $\frac{\$5}{2\ hr}$ 3. $\frac{77\ mi}{3\ hr}$

Skill 3   1. $4.50 per lb   2. 4.8 sales per day   3. 37.3 km per hr

Skill 4   1. TRUE   2. NOT TRUE   3. TRUE

Skill 5   1. 84   2. 23   3. 195

Skill 6   1. 256 (km)   2. 960 (ft)   3. 1728 (dollars)

Unit 12 Test

Skill 1   1. $\frac{7}{100}$; 0.07   2. $\frac{1}{2}$; 0.5   3. $\frac{16}{25}$; 0.64

Skill 2   1. $2\frac{17}{100}$; 2.17   2. 3; 3   3. $5\frac{4}{5}$; 5.8

Skill 3   1. $\frac{13}{2000}$; 0.0065   2. $\frac{1}{600}$; 0.00167   3. $\frac{1}{125}$; 0.008

Skill 4   1. $\frac{57}{80}$; 0.7125   2. $\frac{21}{32}$; 0.65625   3. $2\frac{2}{15}$; 2.1333

Skill 5   1. 8%   2. $23\frac{1}{5}$% or 23.2%   3. $300\frac{7}{10}$% or 300.7%

Skill 6   1. 10%   2. 75%   3. $44\frac{4}{9}$% $\doteq$ 44.4%

Skill 7   1. 550%   2. $487\frac{1}{2}$% or 487.5%   3. $266\frac{2}{3}$% $\doteq$ 266.7%

Skill 8   1. 4.8   2. 165   3. $31.25

Skill 9   1. 62%   2. 172%   3. $22\frac{1}{2}$% or 22.5%

Skill 10   1. 25   2. 40   3. 48

Unit 10 Test

Skill 1	1. 8.73	2. 75.0276	3. 902.006
Skill 2	1. 8.53	2. 5.0	3. 9.840
Skill 3	1. 7.15	2. 0.3125	3. 1.625
Skill 4	1. $\frac{7}{10}$	2. $16\frac{7}{50}$	3. $21\frac{13}{40}$
Skill 5	1. $222.36	2. 137.651	3. 69.723
Skill 6	1. $435.20	2. 251.444	3. 31.634
Skill 7	1. $224.68	2. 554.447	3. 63.28
Skill 8	1. $477.79	2. 176.9908	3. 75.362
Skill 9	1. 90.81	2. 20,219.5	3. 16,569
Skill 10	1. 9.366	2. 84.3102	3. 305,439
Skill 11	1. 0.2	2. 0.505	3. 3.015
Skill 12	1. 8.3	2. 1.5	3. 60.6

Unit 11 Test

Skill 1	1. $\frac{8}{3}$	2. $\frac{8}{3}$	3. $\frac{14}{5}$
Skill 2	1. $\frac{32 \text{ mi}}{5 \text{ hr}}$	2. $\frac{16 \text{ km}}{3 \text{ L}}$	3. $\frac{\$39}{4 \text{ hr}}$
Skill 3	1. 16¢ per lemon	2. 10.7 mi per hr	3. $32.50 per wk
Skill 4	1. TRUE	2. NOT TRUE	3. NOT TRUE
Skill 5	1. 65	2. 24	3. 430
Skill 6	1. 228 (km)	2. 9 (cars)	3. 3360 (dollars)

Unit 12 Test

Skill 1	1. $\frac{9}{100}$; 0.09	2. $\frac{7}{10}$; 0.7	3. $\frac{21}{25}$; 0.84
Skill 2	1. $3\frac{13}{100}$; 3.13	2. 4; 4	3. $6\frac{13}{20}$; 6.65
Skill 3	1. $\frac{9}{2000}$; 0.0045	2. $\frac{1}{500}$; 0.002	3. $\frac{1}{240}$; 0.00417
Skill 4	1. $\frac{43}{80}$; 0.5375	2. $\frac{7}{30}$; 0.23333	3. $1\frac{27}{125}$; 1.216
Skill 5	1. 7%	2. 68.5% or $68\frac{1}{2}$%	3. 401.3% or $401\frac{3}{10}$%
Skill 6	1. 20%	2. $62\frac{1}{2}$% or 62.5%	3. $83\frac{1}{3}$% $\doteq$ 83.3%
Skill 7	1. 220%	2. $216\frac{2}{3}$% $\doteq$ 216.7%	3. $266\frac{2}{3}$% = 266.7%
Skill 8	1. 28.8	2. $154.8	3. 258
Skill 9	1. 45%	2. 115%	3. $12\frac{1}{2}$% or 12.5%
Skill 10	1. 75	2. $60	3. 80

Module C Test

Unit 10 Skills 1–12

1. 215.0233   2. 18.6   3. 6.3   4. $19\frac{13}{20}$ 5. 37.884   6. 20.222   7. 81.218

8. 556.8785   9. 447.64   10. 330.081   11. 29.35   12. 0.75

Unit 11 Skills 1–6

1. $\frac{21}{5}$ 2. $\frac{32 \text{ km}}{3 \text{ L}}$ 3. 11.5 km per min   4. NOT TRUE   5. 11   6. 192 (ft)

Unit 12 Skills 1–10

1. $\frac{12}{25}$; 0.48   2. $4\frac{1}{4}$; 4.25   3. $\frac{1}{250}$; 0.004   4. $\frac{13}{16}$; 0.8125   5. 54.2% or $54\frac{1}{5}$%

6. $31\frac{1}{4}$% or 31.25%   7. 775%   8. 182.75   9. 12%   10. 60

Module C: Evaluation

To the student:

Houghton Mifflin, as a publisher of fine textbooks in mathematics, is constantly working to make good materials even better. We believe that the person best qualified to comment on how to improve a book is the student who has been learning from it. You can help us make better the learning experiences of future students if you will take a moment to share with us your impressions of PERSONALIZED COMPUTATIONAL SKILLS PROGRAM.

The Publisher

ABOUT YOUR COLLEGE

1. In what state is your college located? _____ **2.** How many students? _____

3. What type of college? (2-year, 4-year, public, private, college or university) _____

ABOUT YOUR COURSE

1. Name the course in which PCSP is used: _____

2. Estimate what percent of the entire student body takes this course: _____

3. How long is the course? (1-semester, 2-semester, etc.) _____

4. Does your college give a placement exam in math to entering students? _____

ABOUT YOUR CLASS

1. How many times does your class meet?

	Per Week	Per Term
For Lecture		
For Lab		
For Testing		
Other (Specify)		

2. How many students are in your class section?_____

3. Who is teaching your class? (Professor, Instructor, Graduate Student, etc.)

_____

ABOUT YOURSELF

1. How many years of high school math did you have? _____

2. How long has it been since your last math course?_____

3. How would you rate yourself as a math student? (1.0 Fair to 4.0 Top) _____

4. Are you working? _____ Full time? _____ Part time? _____

5. What is your career goal? _____

ABOUT YOUR BOOK (PERSONALIZED COMPUTATIONAL SKILLS PROGRAM)

1. How would you rate PCSP as a textbook?

	Low	1	2	3	4	5	High
Organization							
Useful Content							
Explanations							
Testing							
Overall Rating							

2. Identify (by page number) any parts of the book that you found especially difficult: _____
_____

3. Do you know of another text that you like better? (Author/Title) _____
_____

4. Will you keep this book for future reference? _____

ABOUT YOUR IDEAS

What changes would you recommend be made to improve this text for future students?

Mail to:

Houghton Mifflin
Attention: Editor-in-Chief
College Mathematics
One Beacon Street
Boston, MA   02107